High Crimes and Misdemeanors
True Crime Stories in the Santa Maria Valley

Lucinda Ransick, Director

With Edward J. Zemaitis

Edited by Michael W. Farris

Santa Maria Valley Historical Society Museum

JANAWAY PUBLISHING INC.
Santa Maria, California

Copyright © 2021, Santa Maria Valley Historical Society

ALL RIGHTS RESERVED.
No part of this publication may be reproduced, stored in a
retrieval system, or transmitted in any form or by any
means whatsoever, whether electronic, mechanical,
magnetic recording, or photocopying, without the
prior written approval of the Copyright holder
or Publisher, excepting brief quotations
for inclusion in book reviews.

Author: Lucinda Ransick
With Edward J. Zemaitis

Published for Santa Maria Valley Historical Society

Edited by Michael W. Farris

Published by:

Janaway Publishing, Inc.
732 Kelsey Ct.
Santa Maria, California 93454
(805) 925-1952
www.janawaygenealogy.com

2021

Library of Congress Control Number: 2021953225

ISBN: 978-1-59641-466-2

Cover Photo c.1885 Identified as Uncle Tony: Policeman and Deputy Sheriff in Santa Barbara County

Copies of this book may be purchased from the Santa Maria Valley Historical Society
616 S. Broadway, Santa Maria, CA 93454

Made in the United States of America

Dedicated to Bruno J. (Joe) Zemaitis
(January 10, 1917- November 6, 2004)

Bruno Joseph Zemaitis, born in the coal mining town of Minden, West Virginia, was delivered by the company doctor for the New River Pocahontas Coal Company. He grew up in the company town, where his father, Joseph, worked as a coal miner, and his mother, Ursula, worked to raise and care for six children.

In 1927, the family moved to Chicago and joined the Lithuanian community near Halstead Street. During the Great Depression, the family lost its savings when the banks closed. Bruno and his brother, Bill, worked in a machine shop. One shift, a piece of metal flew off a bending break and killed the man standing next to Bruno; that day he borrowed five dollars and left for California.

With the business card of a cement mason in Los Angeles in his pocket, he arrived in California and learned the masonry trade. During World War II, he worked for Howard Hughes building aircraft. After the war, he ventured north to Santa Maria. He sold Mac Tools during the day and worked as a relief patrolman for the Merchant's Patrol Service at night. This became his passion, and soon he was able to purchase that business with a $500 handshake-loan from Frank Shields at Bank of America. Over the next 57 years, Bruno built Overland Investigation Bureau into a staple of the Santa Maria Valley.

The Snappy Lunch was a local café with a horseshoe counter, complete with table-top jukeboxes, which offered lunch, dinner, and breakfast to those working late hours. Bruno was in the habit of stopping for coffee during his nightly rounds. He met Elizabeth "Beth" Harding who was working at the café located at Cook and Broadway. He and Beth raised a family: Ron, Jim, Mike, and Jeanette. Jim went on to manage Overland and continues to this writing.

Bruno had a distinguished career in security and crime investigation. He worked some major cases including the Wray homicide case in Santa Maria and the death of Betty Short, the *Black Dahlia*, in Los Angeles. Most personal was a local case in which he shot and killed Benjamin James, a career criminal sought by state authorities, during a burglary at the Santa Maria High School in 1950.

Working at the cutting edge of his profession, in 1961, Bruno attended classes at Long Beach College on how to effectively deploy a new technology in crime fighting, the Polygraph Lie Detector. He was one of the first civilians in the state to do so. Throughout his life, he continued to encourage professionalism in his industry. He was a founding member of the California Association of Private Investigators. He was well known for his efforts in crime prevention. Would-be felons were known to "steer clear" of Bruno's security clients.

Throughout his career Bruno was assisted in his efforts by Beth, an able administrator, until her passing in 1996. She was his able "right hand man," often donning a uniform, returning to handle administration, then preparing dinner for the family.

Bruno remained active in the daily operation of Overland until he passed in his sleep in 2004.

Acknowledgements

Special thanks to Norm Hays and Jason Blanco, research assistants on the book. Both contributed hours to "digging deep" to ensure the most accurate portrayal of each case, whether it involved weapons or pictorial representations, these gentlemen made a significant contribution. Also to Charla Chaffee and Lana Knor for photo searches and obituaries! On a daily basis these gals keep the society and museum going.

Table of Contents

Dedicated to Bruno J. (Joe) Zemaitis iii
Acknowledgements iv
Introduction 1
    The Second Amendment 1
    Our Scope of Work 1
Chapter 1: Vigilante Justice 3
    Salomon Maria Simeon Pico 5
    John A. Power 6
    Pio Linares 8
    Walter Thurtell-Murray 9
    Captain David Patrick Mallagh 13
    Jehu 14
    Bill Hudson's Saloon 15
    Michael Mullee 16
    The Santa Maria Vigilantes 17
    Small Arms of the 1800s 18
        The Rifle 19
        The Revolver 20
    Lynching in Santa Maria 20
        Edmund Luther Criswell 21
        Trinidad German 24
    Forensics of a Legal Hanging 24
    Gunfights of the West 25
        Miller-Stokes Duel 26
Chapter 2: Child Murder and Child Murderers 28
    Solomon Hill Sniper: Michael Andrew Clark, 16 28
    Forensics Science before 1960 32
    Harry Eckland Blochman Case 34
    Edward Walker: Killer Kid 39
    Wray Case 40
    Eileen Effie Baker Case 43
    Dystiny McKenna Myers 46

    First-Degree Murder 47

    Statistically Speaking 49

Chapter 3: Domestic Violence 51

    Haslam-Low Case 52

    Epps Case 53

    Schlager Case 53

    Hunt-Throckmorton Case 55

    Brian Keith Reid 58

    Leopoldo Ramiro "Joe" Foxen 60

    John Logan "Buddy" Spears 61

Chapter 4: Suicide-Self Murder 62

    Murad Jacob "Jack" Kevorkian 62

    Ross Leonard (Scott) Galyon 64

    Robert Patrick Foxen 64

    Floyd Sutherland Teachout 65

    Santa Maria Woman Attempts Suicide 66

    Filippo Frusconi Rusconi 66

    Does a Violent Death in a House have to be Disclosed? 66

Chapter 5: Unsolved Cases-Cold Cases 68

    The Black Dahlia 68

    J. Charles Collins 75

    The Case of Robert Lee Lopez 75

Chapter 6: Cold Blooded Murder 78

    The Robert Taylor Bailey Case 79

    Thomas Clayton Hilton Case 80

    James M. Noriega: Triple Homicide 81

Chapter 7: Missing-Exploited-Abused 83

    Hobo 83

    Kidnapping of Ben Stowell 84

    Lane Elwood Bryant 86

    Michael Jackson Acquitted 87

    James Harrison Gamble 89

    Hans Jorgen Kardel 90

Chapter 8: Arson 92

    Santa Maria Fire Department 92
    Japan Town Fire 93
    Thanksgiving Weekend Fire 93
    Bradley Hotel Fire 94
    House Fires 95
    Bruce Horner 97
    Robert Scott Forsythe 97
    Town Center Inn Fire October 12, 2013 98

Chapter 9: Evolution of Law Enforcement 100
    First Justice in Our Valley, January 1846 100
    Miranda 101
    Ernesto A. Miranda, The Man 103
    POST: Commission on Peace Officer Standards and Training 103
    Private Investigators and Security 104
    Benjamin Fredrick James 105
    Keith Bennett 106
    Defund the Police 106
        Santa Maria Chiefs of Police 107

Chapter 10: Misdemeanors 108

Epilogue 110
    Crime Scene Cleanup 110

References 111

Introduction

Human history must take recon on the topic of crime and punishment. How we develop as a society the rules under which we all agree to exist is fundamental to building a community. While no one enjoys the scrutiny of judgement, most of us will admit to the need to establish a baseline of reasonable, acceptable behavior for the whole and the good of mankind. The Mayflower Compact* was such an agreement. As humans, we can all admit that without rules, there is no order. It is the nature of man to have order. It is precisely how we define it that creates the bumps in the road.

Most consider the core of law and order to be the right to self-defense. A claim of self-defense can exonerate one from what otherwise might be a crime. From almost the beginning of mankind itself, there has been a system that dictates acceptable and unacceptable civil behavior. The first policing organization was created in Egypt about 3000 BCE. The pharaoh appointed an official who was responsible for justice and security.

In the United States on September 24, 1789, the United States Congress created the first federal law enforcement officer, the United States Marshal. President George Washington appointed thirteen U.S. Marshals.

The Second Amendment

The second Amendment to the United State Constitution states: **"A well-regulated Militia, being necessary to the security of a free State, the right of the people to keep and bear Arms, shall not be infringed."**

The Second Amendment to the United States Constitution protects the right to keep and bear arms. It was ratified on December 15, 1791, along with nine other articles of the Bill of Rights. The Second Amendment was proposed by James Madison to allow the creation of civilian forces that can counteract a tyrannical federal government. The right to keep and bear arms in the United States is a fundamental right.

Our Scope of Work

This is a look at how the Santa Maria Valley and Santa Barbara County, which had original jurisdiction over the valley, adjudicated justice.

---

* IN THE NAME OF GOD, AMEN. We, whose names are underwritten, the Loyal Subjects of our dread Sovereign Lord King *James*, by the Grace of God, of *Great Britain*, *France*, and *Ireland*, King, *Defender of the Faith*, etc. Having undertaken for the Glory of God, and Advancement of the Christian Faith, and the Honour of our King and Country, a Voyage to plant the first Colony in the northern Parts of *Virginia*; Do by these Presents, solemnly and mutually, in the Presence of God and one another, covenant and combine ourselves together into a civil Body Politick, for our better Ordering and Preservation, and Furtherance of the Ends aforesaid: And by Virtue hereof do enact, constitute, and frame, such just and equal Laws, Ordinances, Acts, Constitutions, and Offices, from time to time, as shall be thought most meet and convenient for the general Good of the Colony; unto which we promise all due Submission and Obedience. IN WITNESS whereof we have hereunto subscribed our names at *Cape-Cod* the eleventh of November, in the Reign of our Sovereign Lord King *James*, of *England*, *France*, and *Ireland*, the eighteenth, and of *Scotland* the fifty-fourth, *Anno Domini*; 1620.

Chapter 1: Vigilante Justice

There has always been some form of mob law enforcement. In fact, it still exists today visible in national headlines. Gun fights and the hanging of horse thieves in the Old West provide some exciting early imagery. Today, it is riots and the destruction of property. These demonstrations of civil disobedience can be more accurately dubbed vigilante justice. Vigilante justice describes the actions of a single person or group of people who claim to enforce the law but lack any legitimate authority to do so.

The word vigilante brings to mind what became known as "frontier justice," law and order on a violent frontier where the need for law enforcement preceded an established legal system. Men banded together to more safely accomplish community obligations by punishing those who transgressed the laws of property (stolen livestock) or person (rape and murder). Men formed a posse and delivered swift justice to the guilty often at the end of a rope, lynching.

The word lynching paints a picture of impromptu justice without the benefit of legal proceedings. Hanging, in other terms, is that form of execution that was the most popular, legal and extralegal, way of putting criminals to death in the United States from its inception. Brought to the American Colonies by English ancestors, the method actually originated in Persia (modern Iran) about 2,500 years ago. Hanging became the method of choice for most countries as it produced a highly visible deterrent with the public invited to view the spectacle! Viewers came from far and wide to watch, looking to the gallows or tree to see punishment meted out to wrong-doers. Legal hangings, practiced by the early American colonists, were readily accepted by the public as a proper form of punishment for serious crimes.

Most hangings were carried out by the sheriff or legal entity of the town or county where the death sentence had been passed. Prisoner's deaths were usually painful as most executioners were not expert enough to know how to calculate the correct drop of the hangman's noose to ensure breaking the neck. Thus, the individual usually died by strangulation. The use of gallows with a trap door did not become common practice until the 1870s. Before that, most were hanged from a tree branch, being turned off the back of a cart, or from a horse.

Vigilantes were encouraged to pursue frontier justice by big bounties; $100 in 1858 is equivalent in purchasing power to about $3,000 today. In 1860, laborers made about 10 cents an hour, about $300 per year. Privates in the Union army earned $11 a week.

Henry J. Dalley

The 1850s was a turbulent age in California. The Gold Rush attracted tens of thousands of fortune seekers, many unsavory. The conclusion of the Mexican-American War in 1848 shattered the ruling order and brought in new generations of Anglo settlers to challenge the longstanding Spanish customs and property claims of the Californios, who had prospered under Mexican governance. Lawlessness, public drunkenness, and violence prevailed in many quarters, including remote San Luis Obispo and Santa Barbara Counties, where vigilante committees were formed to enforce law and order. Murder and lynching were commonplace. Many residents never went to sleep without a revolver under their pillow. This decade was often referred to as the "bloody fifties." Elected in April 1850 as the first sheriff of San Luis Obispo, Henry J. Dalley resigned one year later stating the job was "too dangerous!"

The original Santa Maria town builders were arriving late in the 1860s. A lot of the unlawfulness had been quelled, but vigilantism had benefitted these budding communities. Unsavory sorts could be dealt with quickly by the righteous, hardworking citizens. Sworn law officers were still not abundant. Justice was slow unless residents decided differently. Mob justice was always simmering just under the surface.

Stagecoach robbery was one of the most difficult crimes to solve. Perpetrators almost always got away with it. Masks made accurate identification virtually impossible. California stagecoach runs were popular targets as there was gold ore being transported to secure institutions and payroll for the railroads. In early days, payments were made in cold hard currency, so a lot of it could be traveling the open roads at any given moment. Vigilante justice thrived along the bumpy meandering trails. One of the first horse drawn stage robberies recorded was in 1856 and the last about 1913. Over that period there were nearly 500 reported attacks on stages and hundreds more on small parties of cowboys traversing the west from north to south.

Long grades like this made for easy hold-ups.

Across the western frontier, highwaymen robbed small groups of riders and stagecoaches with near impunity. Stage coaches were often hit by selecting a site where the stagecoach would have to slow down. Thus, a stage driver knew to be especially careful at certain locations along his route. Since horses were involved, there was a schedule of stops for the stages to provide humane care for the animals and a break for the humans bouncing behind. This well-established path gave outlaws the means to target the easiest place to hold-up a stagecoach.

One such place, later named for its bandit, is Solomon Grade. Solomon Grade is located about 9 miles south of Santa Maria, 3.7 miles south of the Clark Avenue over-pass at Highway 101. The bandit, Salomon Pico, was using this avenue before there was a town that would be Santa Maria. The roadway, coming from both the north at Clark Avenue and the south at Cat Canyon Road, rises slowly over 3.5-miles to the pass at 944 feet above sea level making the climb from either side about 350 feet in 3.7 miles. Today's automobile will never notice the grade, but a bicyclist will tell you it's there. A stagecoach driver would likely have rested his team at least once, if not twice, before reaching the crest. This made the stretch the perfect location for outlaws to await their prey.

Salomon Maria Simeon Pico

Born September 5, 1821, Pico was a Californio and a cousin of former governor Pío Pico. Salomon led a bandit band in the counties of the central coast of California in the early years following the Mexican-American War. Pico was considered by Californios to be a patriot, especially those who contested the American conquest of Alta California, and vehemently opposed its subsequent incorporation into the United States. Pico was hated for his lawlessness by the newly arrived Americans but protected by the Californios as a defender of the people.

Salomon Pico is said to have vowed revenge against the American interlopers. Avoiding the gold fields for his marauding, he moved to the vicinity of Rancho Los Alamos in Santa Barbara County. By day, he was a stock dealer, trading in horses and cattle.

Formerly in southern California, cattle were raised mostly for their hides, but now there was a high demand for food in the northern gold and silver mines. The price of cattle soared making it very profitable to drive these same cattle to northern markets. Cowboys and purchasing agents would ride south with large amounts of gold dust to buy stock, then drive them north to sell for a profit. Salomon Pico placed himself propitiously along their route. In the dark of night, Pico and his gang would wait in ambush. Consisting of only two or three, many of these cattle traders were never heard of after passing San Luis Obispo. Much later, numbers of human skeletons were found, with a bullet hole in the skull, in the countryside accounting for their mysterious disappearances. The victims were Americans whom the Californios felt were their enemies, and a conspiracy of silence enveloped Pico and his gang's crimes; they were never divulged by the locals. On the occasion that one member of the gang was brought to trial, the result was an acquittal. In this region, the Californios were still in the majority, and Pico was connected to its influential members. The gang avoided conflicts with county officials, who in turn seemed to let the bandits alone.

It is not known exactly what happened to all the gold Pico took, but it is known that his popularity soared very quickly among his own people. By 1851 he was fully established as a flamboyant outlaw with a loyal gang and a following among his people. He had become so popular that it was said with a knock on the door and an urgent request for harbor, he could ride his horse straight away into a person's some and thus elude the pursuit of any posse. It is legendary stories like this that have led to the romanticism and speculation of Pico as the original Zorro.

Pico narrowly escaped vigilante justice after the murder of a mail rider. A party of volunteers pursued the gang and, near San Luis Obispo, captured a group of men that included Salomon

Pico narrowly escaped vigilante justice after the murder of a mail rider. A party of volunteers pursued the gang and, near San Luis Obispo, captured a group of men that included Salomon Pico. These men were tried at a vigilante court and were sentenced to be hanged. Before the sentence could be executed, civil authorities rescued them. Pico, because of the standing of his cousin Pío Pico in the community, was freed on bail. The other captured Californios were also released on various pretexts. One American, William Otis Hall, remained in custody. On the night of August 9, vigilantes broke into the jail and enforced their ruling. Otis was hanged on the door of the jail becoming the first known lynch mob victim on the central coast. Pico quickly fled the region.

In the mid-1850s, Pico became a somewhat permanent resident of Baja California. He boasted to any who would listen that he had killed 39 "yankees" during his Alta California days. In 1856 he stabbed an Englishman to death in a La Paz restaurant under the mistaken notion that he was a Yankee. Pico's life came to an end in May 1860 when he and several other suspected outlaws were executed by firing squad.

Members of his gang, as well as others, continued to plague the central coast region for many years under new leaders like Pio Linares and Jack Powers.

John A. Power

> Death of Jack Powers. — The telegraph brings intelligence of the death of the notorious Jack Powers, who committed so many murders and robberies in the southern country in the spring of 1857. He was murdered near Tubac, Arizona, by his Mexican peons. Served him right.
>
> Visalia Weekly Sun, Nov 1860

Born in Ireland in 1827 as John A. Power, he came to the United States with his parents in 1836, and settled with them in New York City. John was 19 years old when the Mexican-American War began in 1846. The New York Volunteers was a military unit organized by Colonel Jonathan D. Stevenson to occupy and settle California; men in the unit were promised land in the region should the war be successful.

After the war, John Power became known as Jack Powers, a gambler, and had both reputation bruises and decorations as a result of his continued time in Santa Barbara County. He acted equally as villain and law enforcement officer (leading a posse seeking and punishing law breakers). Like many men of his time, he was no angel and was, at times, the bad man.

> JACK POWERS.— Former news from Sonora announced the death of Jack Powers, somewhat notorious in California. Jack had a ranch near the line and, it is supposed, was killed by his peons. His body was so much mutilated by hogs as to be scarcely recognisable; and from appearances, it is supposed he was killed by a blow from behind with an axe.
>
> The Daily Bee, November 1860

A group of vigilantes on the Central Coast believed Jack Powers was secretly the leader of an outlaw gang of highway-robbers and murderers of victims and witnesses associated with his crimes. The gang operated for several years beginning in the fall of 1853. Taking on the route abandoned in southern and central California by Pico's original band, Powers and his bandits were accused by various local vigilante groups of numerous robberies and murders that had been committed on the stretch of El Camino Real running north through San Luis Obispo County, making it the most dangerous route in the state. Powers eventually fled to Sonora to escape a Los Angeles lynch mob.

*On the basis of the accusations leveled by a group of San Luis Obispo vigilantes, on May 31, 1858, Governor John B. Weller issued rewards for the arrests of the gang members still at large:

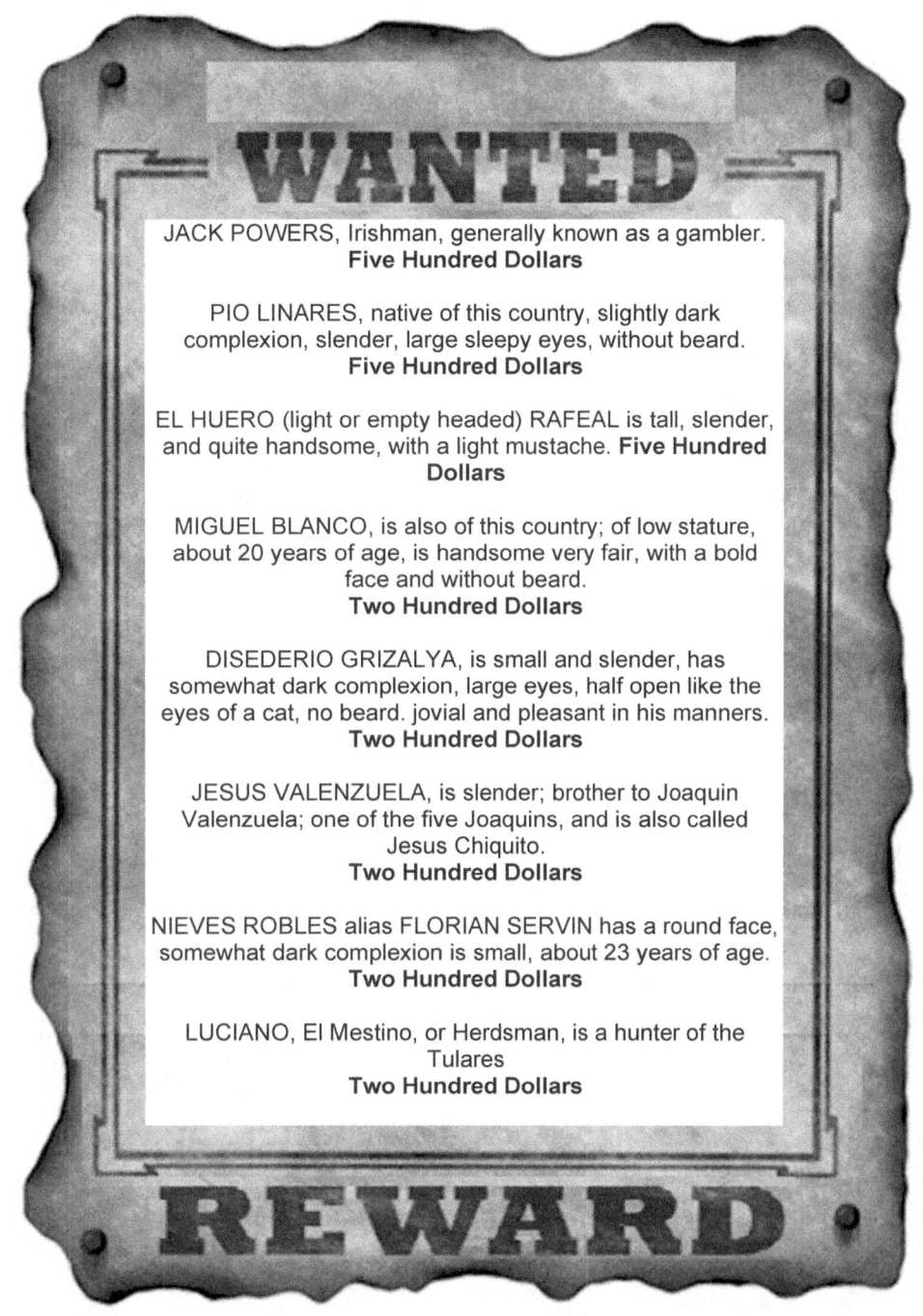

WANTED

JACK POWERS, Irishman, generally known as a gambler.
Five Hundred Dollars

PIO LINARES, native of this country, slightly dark complexion, slender, large sleepy eyes, without beard.
Five Hundred Dollars

EL HUERO (light or empty headed) RAFEAL is tall, slender, and quite handsome, with a light mustache. **Five Hundred Dollars**

MIGUEL BLANCO, is also of this country; of low stature, about 20 years of age, is handsome very fair, with a bold face and without beard.
Two Hundred Dollars

DISEDERIO GRIZALYA, is small and slender, has somewhat dark complexion, large eyes, half open like the eyes of a cat, no beard. jovial and pleasant in his manners.
Two Hundred Dollars

JESUS VALENZUELA, is slender; brother to Joaquin Valenzuela; one of the five Joaquins, and is also called Jesus Chiquito.
Two Hundred Dollars

NIEVES ROBLES alias FLORIAN SERVIN has a round face, somewhat dark complexion is small, about 23 years of age.
Two Hundred Dollars

LUCIANO, El Mestino, or Herdsman, is a hunter of the Tulares
Two Hundred Dollars

REWARD

---

* WHEREAS, IT IS REPRESENTED to me by the citizens of San Luis Obispo that several atrocious murders and robberies have recently been perpetrated and that upon the oath, of respectable men, these crimes have been charged upon the following persons, who are still at large: Now, therefore, by virtue of the power vested in me, by Constitution and laws of this State I hereby offer these REWARDS for their arrest and conviction. Done at Sacramento, California, this 31st day of May, A. D., One Thousand Eight Hundred and Fifty-Eight. In witness whereof I have hereunto set my hand, and affixed the Great Seal of the State. JOHN B. WELLER. Attest: Ferris Forman, Secretary of State.

Pio Linares

As the bad seed of the Linares clan, Pio took up with an infamous gang of bandits led by Jack Powers. In the mid-1850s, the stretch between Santa Barbara and San Luis Obispo was the most dangerous road in California as Jack Powers and Pio Linares carried out a string of murders and hold-ups, dumping the bodies of their victims on the roadside. Corpses where a common sight. San Luis Obispo Sheriff Francisco Castro was outgunned by the Powers-Linares highwaymen. The gun-slinging Pio Linares, known as *el pistolero*, soon topped the list of most wanted in San Luis Obispo. His motto was "Dead men tell no tales."

Pio Linares. From San Diego History Center

Promptly taking the law into their own hands and led by a dapper young attorney named Walter Murray (below), the citizens of San Luis Obispo formed a vigilante committee of 150 armed men. The volunteers swore a vow to rid the county of Pio and his desperadoes, which the Santa Barbara Gazette branded a "ruthless band of assassins." Pio merely taunted the vigilantes claiming his gang was stronger. On June 13, 1858, sixty to eighty members of the Committee of Vigilance surrounded the adobe house at Rancho Cañada de los Osos, where Pio was hiding out, and burned it to the ground. Pio and his desperadoes escaped into the woods.

MEMORIAL

Inscription

Sacred
to the memory of
John Matlack
A native of Steubenville
Ohio
Who was killed June 12
1858
in assistng to arrest a
band of assassins.
Age 22 Years
He died doing his duty.

The next morning, Pio and two of his followers were cornered in a stand of willow trees. In the rapid exchange of gunfire, Walter Murray was wounded in the arm and vigilante John Matlack was mortally wounded. Pio fell dead in the storm of bullets. His two cronies were captured and hanged the next day. By the time the vigilante committee was disbanded, it had hanged no fewer than six suspected outlaws.

Walter Thurtell-Murray

Vigilantes are generally unnamed as they usually operating outside the law themselves. Walter T. Murray is an exception to this rule.

Walter Murray (9 Dec 1826, London - 5 Oct 1875, California), was a printer, miner, lawyer, and finally a Judge of the District Court of San Luis Obispo, California. For a time, he was also the publisher of the San Luis Obispo *Tribune* newspaper.

Walter had some legal training as a youth in England. In August 1843, at the age of 17, He embarked for the United States arriving in Boston aboard the *Velasco* on September 28, 1843. He gained experience in the printing trade in Boston as a compositor for a Mr. Turner at 27 Brighton Street.

After living in Boston and New York, in August 1846 Walter enlisted as a volunteer in the Stevenson Regiment towards the end of the Mexican War (as did John A. Powers). Having travelled from New York around the Horn and seen action in Baja California, Mexico, he arrived in California on October 21, 1847. When the regiment was disbanded in 1848, he moved on to gold rush country; in the mines, he made the acquaintance of Romualdo Pacheco, future Governor of California, who was a native of San Luis Obispo.

In 1851 near what is now Yosemite National Park, at the foot of the Sierra Nevada mountains, in the town of Sonora, Walter became proprietor, with his former companion in arms, James O'Sullivan, of the first newspaper in Tuolumne County, the Sonora "Herald." Here in 1850, he had been joined by his young brother Alexander, who then also assisted with the newspaper.

In 1853, Walter settled in San Luis Obispo, where he was admitted to the Bar and established a law practice. The Walter Murray adobe still stands in a park at 747 Monterey Street, opposite the SLO County Historical Museum and the Mission church. On the other side, the park is bounded by San Luis Creek. The SLO Chamber of Commerce points out that the 1849 "white-washed building at the end of Mission Plaza in San Luis Obispo is all that remains of the adobe home of Walter Murray." He "printed the first copies of San Luis Obispo's local newspaper, *The Tribune*" in the home, which is still on the "San Luis Obispo Path of History."

Walter's was the first name on an 1858 Vigilance Committee roster, and he took a leading role in hunting down the bandits who had committed murder on the Rancho San Juan Capistrano. During a skirmish with Pio Linares and his gang, Walter was shot in the arm.

Walter Murray ran for political office, was appointed District Judge of the First Judicial District (the counties of San Luis Obispo and Santa Barbara) in December 1873, and was about to be formally elected to that office when he died of gastritis on October 5th, 1875.

Of great interest is his first hand writing of his encounter with the desperado, Pio Linares. It varies somewhat from other published accounts. What follows is an excerpt from a letter to his sister Ann dated May 1858, San Luis Obispo.

> "You have heard of robberies and assassinations in this country. You have perhaps deemed newspaper accounts of them to be mere exaggerations. We here

have lately passed through realities which shame fiction. You must know that the Southern Counties of California are cattle districts. From thence are drawn the large bands of cattle which supply the great bulk of the population of this country. Numbers of men make it their business to bring down money and horses from San Francisco and the mines, buy cattle here and below and drive them up. As these men are from one to three months away from home and travel from three to six hundred miles and back, their disappearance does not excite comment for a long time. Hence ever since 1849 it has been a common thing for such men to be laid in wait for and murdered for their money. Long before I came to San Luis, this place was celebrated for such occurrences. Scarcely three months have passed without the discovery at some point or another within 40 miles of here, of from one to three skeletons or corpses.

"It has always been rumored that some of the evil-doers were residents of San Luis, and were protected by the native families. One man in particular, one Pio Linares, a young man of 21, married to a widow of the name of Maria Antonia, was suspected of these crimes. And yet this Pio and his wife ever since I have been here have been admitted into the native society almost on a par with the best of them. Men whispered, but they held out the hand of fellowship; they visited them and invited them and all passed off. Of one thing however, I can assure you, namely, that neither I nor my wife had anything to do with these wretches, for I had my eye on them from the first. The fellow had everybody scared. One day he would draw his pistol on one man, tomorrow his knife on another. Today he would bully this man, tomorrow that, and no one dared to prosecute him. However, the Americans here and I among them kept up a continual talk about him and determined as soon as we could throw light on his movements to bring him to account. In the meantime, we all had to keep a good lookout, so much so, that several of us at different times were in great risk from him and his native followers.

"At length, in last December, two Basque Frenchmen, going up with cattle disappeared, and one was found a day or two afterwards killed with pistol-balls. The other was not found. All stood aghast because no proof could be had and the infernal natives stood together to shield their suspected countrymen. I myself, although anxious to hang a dozen of them, defended the culprit who was arrested on suspicion. There was no evidence hardly against him. He turned out afterwards to be the spy or servant of the assassin party. The principals, including Pio Linares, flourished around town, danced at our balls, bullied our citizens, and when it was whispered that he was guilty, openly dared us to the proof; and offered to fight whoever should attempt it.

"I was in a ticklish position. My client, Nieves Robles, would have confessed all to me had I pressed him - he was so frightened, but I did not dare do it. My life would not have been safe from the main villains. Public opinion among this bastard people was not strong enough to have sustained me, and I might have been off before my time, and none to have said "God help him". I cleared the man, or rather the astuteness of the villains in leaving no witness of their guilt, cleared him and at the same time I and many other Americans resolved to act when the time should come. Law could not help us. Law could not force a confession from a criminal. And law was powerless anyhow before a jury of Californians. A few short months and the time arrived.

"On the 12th of May, only a fortnight before I commenced this letter, a party of eight men, two of whom were accomplices in the murder above accounted, went to the rancho of San Juan Capistrano, where two Frenchmen named Baratie and Borel, had recently settled, about 40 miles from here, and made a general attack upon the premises. They murdered both the Frenchmen, and one of them carried off Baratie's wife, a countrywoman of my wife's - forced her to submit to his embraces, and finally accompanied her to a place of safety after a week's travel through a wilderness. The plan was to lay [the] murder upon two servants of the Frenchmen, Californians, who were to have been murdered at a distance from the house, where their bodies could not be found. The two men, however, who were charged with this part of the plot spared the servants' lives, without informing their comrades that they had done so. The result was that one of the servants went to the nearest rancho and informed Capt. Mallagh, a friend of mine, of the murder, when he immediately saddled up and brought word to me. The spoil obtained at this murder was $2700, besides watches and jewelry. It was divided up between the men before the eyes of the owners.

"When Mallagh brought me the news I took the servants' deposition and got out warrants to arrest eight persons, names unknown. In the meantime, the villains, as usual, had returned to town, thinking that no trace had been left behind of their guilt. One of them *[Santos Peralta]* was recognized by the witness and immediately clapped in jail. The rest fled. That night we visited the jail and endeavored to make the assassin disclose his accomplices. He was silent as the grave. We left him hanging from the roof of his cell. His countrymen cried innocent but we afterwards learned that he was the very one who had killed M. Baratie before his wife's eyes.

"In the morning a party of 15 men started in pursuit. They caught sight of the villains and recognized four of them but they escaped by leaving their horses and taking to the brush. The party staid out about eight days, returning with one prisoner, unconnected with the late murder but an old and hardened offender, one Joaquin Valenzuela.

"This Pio Linares, the head villain, had not taken part in the last murder having returned before getting to the house on account of his horse throwing and hurting him. This man remained in his house with his wife while our party was in search of the others, trusting to his long impunity. Our party, however, had resolved to take him, and on their return, before coming into town, and before anyone knew of their approach, they surrounded his house, at about 3 o'clock, A.M. and demanded his surrender. He refused to give up whereupon they set fire to his roof, and on his running greeted him with a shower of balls. I have his rifle now, which he carried in his hand. The stock is riddled with balls and buckshot, but he remained uninjured.

"That day we formed a Vigilance Committee and hanged our prisoner, Joaquin Valenzuela, in broad daylight, before the united people of San Luis. The most respectable Americans, Italians, and Spaniards forming our Executive Committee of 12. All the Americans and foreigners formed the body of the general committee. Only two Californians joined. The biggest rancheros, however, furnished us with money, arms and horses.

"We now knew all our men. Six men were implicated in the first murder, eight in the second. Two of them were in both, making a round dozen in all. We offered a reward of $3000 for their delivery, dead or alive and a proportionate part for each. Parties were sent out in different directions. The first man that was brought in was Luciano Tapia, the Mesteno, or wild man- he who had taken off the woman. By this time, we had sent to San Francisco and brought her down. She recognized him. He confessed his guilt. The priest was called to him - he received absolution and was strung up summarily.

"The next man brought in was one of the actors in the first murder José Antonio Garcia. The head conspirator of all, an Irish-American Gambler and horse-racer Jack Powers- well known in Santa Barbara, had inveigled him into the murder. He maintained that he had fired no shot, although he confessed that he saw it done, and got $200 for his share of the booty. He too was strung up.

"Then we had a lull. Half our men were out hunting these fellows at a distance, and no results. At length, last Tuesday, came intelligence that one had been seen in a willow grove at Capt. Wilson's rancho, nine miles from here. Thirty men, of whom I was one, saddled up on the instant and proceeded thither. We hunted all morning unsuccessfully on horseback. In the afternoon I proposed dismounting and searching into the wood on foot. We did so and in an hour's time we came across three horses, two saddles and a bag of provisions, just inside the edge of the wood. We found where they had been trying to make a well. We took their horses etc. and we tried to set fire to the wood, but with little success. The rascals were then quietly waiting for us a little inside, lying down on their bellies, with their pistols cocked. Here every rascal carries his Colt's revolver - a tremendous weapon.

"I offered to follow up the trail with six men but was over ruled. It was getting late and it was agreed to guard the wood till morning. Guards were placed on all sides. That night one of our guards received a shot through the instep. No other shots fired. Next morning, we went into the woods again following up the trails. It was so dense that we were obliged to crawl on our bellies. We found the saddle bags of Pio Linares, the man whose roof had been burned off. In them we found a spy-glass, used to spy out the whereabouts of his victims, some powder, balls and shot, his frock coat and clean linen, needles and thread, and his wife's daguerreotype. While the rest were overhauling these things, I and another man pushed [on] a few more paces and as luck would have it received the first fire. I got shot through the fleshy part of my left arm, and my companion had the whole back of his coat ripped open with a rifle-ball. I could only see what I took to be a man's head, at which I fired three shots from my revolver. One shot went through Pio Linares's leg, slight wound, and another through his coat, and another through the hat I was firing at. The two last shots I fired after being wounded. The robbers fired about 6 or 8 times. We were only about 15 yards from them and in good sight. I then began to feel faint from my wound and backed out. This led to the retiring of the whole party, who then took up a position on the outside to prevent egress. I went home and wrote letters all over the county. By night the wood was surrounded by over 100 men. In the morning Capt. Mallagh with 24 men entered again and after crawling over a mile again drew fire. They had a bush fight of about ten minutes, resulting in the death of one of our party, an American, and the severe wounding of two others, one by accident. Pio Linares was killed, shot through the head, and two others, Miguel Blanco and Desiderio Grijalva, were taken prisoners. This happened on Saturday last.

"On Sunday the American was buried with all the honors of the Catholic Church, which, however were denied to the dead robber, as he refused to listen to the priest in his last agony. He was truly a devilish man and did most of the fighting. If he had not been killed so soon we should have lost several more men. As it was, our loss was surprisingly small. We gave the American a very decent burial - the best ever had in San Luis. 150 men and 30 ladies followed it. That day we took the confessions of the culprits. Both confessed fully. Next day they were both hanged on the same gallows, publicly as usual. Thus we have now a result of six men hanged and one shot in a month's time - all proved participators in murder. This is a result which the law could not have obtained in San Luis in ten years. We are in hot pursuit of another and expect two more down in the next steamer from San Francisco. All are bound to swing as soon as they come into our hands. All the County officers are with us and there is no opposition whatever. All this you will say is horrible, and it is so, but it is necessary and we have no other way to defend our lives and property. The Californians have cowed down, and even are so candid as to acknowledge their countrymen's guilt and the justice of their punishment. Not one man as yet has suffered who was not either [a] participator or aiding and abetting it. The best commentary on this whole matter, however, is that it is a mighty unpleasant business and I wish I lived where I could be free from so terrible a necessity."

Captain David Patrick Mallagh

David P. Mallagh was an Irish immigrant, born 1825 in Kilkeel, Down, Northern Ireland, who became a stock-raiser in San Luis Obispo County. As such he had an interest in purging the area of the bandits who ravaged the route along El Camino Real. He died in his bed on his birthday at age 55 at the state prison in San Quentin where he was one of the guards. An autopsy revealed his cause of death as an enlarged heart. He came to San Luis County about 1853 from Sonoma County.

Land Grant (Acquisition)
23 APR 1853 • San Luis Obispo, California, USA

Acquired a portion of Rancho Pismo from Isaac J. Sparks for $18,500 (see attachment).

1 Source

Jehu

What's in a name? While the bandits and highwaymen where being heralded in the press as frontier Robin Hoods, although gaining less notoriety, there were other men who drove stagecoaches behind mighty horses and grabbed some headlines, the Jehu. Originally a commander of chariots for Ahab, king of Israel, Jehu later led a revolt against the throne and became king himself. In the Bible, it is noted of Jehu that "he drives furiously." In the 17th century, English speakers began using *jehu* as a generic term meaning "coachman."

Photo of Wes Froom, Santa Maria Valley Historical Museum archives

Pioneer drivers of note were Charlie Patterson, Johnny Waugh, John Coleman, Sam Butterfield, Tom Edgar and a character known as "Old Cooper." While the romance of storytelling focused on the bandits, these jehus would tell you that the weather and road conditions posed as much danger and were more unpredictable. Stories at stage stops included tales of these reinsmen. They had to make split second decisions. Jehu Wesley Froom was halted one bright moonlit night about a mile-and-a-half south of La Graciosa. He had a pistol in his belt but was persuaded not to use it. The hold-up man appeared to be accompanied by two accomplices squatting behind the protection of scrub cover behind, and on either side, of the road. The masked man called, "Don't shoot unless I give the signal." Froom could make out their forms and the length of their rifles but not much else. The order was given to toss down the box, a Wells-Fargo box. Froom obeyed. He was then ordered to drive on but not look back under threat that the men wielding the Winchesters were crack marksmen. Froom returned the next morning with the sheriff showing him the scene of the crime and explaining the challengers he faced. Unfortunately, he had the embarrassing opportunity to face down the threat of the previous night as Froom and the sheriff found two dummies made of gunnysacks stuffed with sagebrush and their sharpshooting broom handles jutting from the brush exactly where Froom had spied them!

Hunted stagecoach bandits in early days, Sheriff Charles E. Sherman 1880-1882

Bill Hudson's Saloon

In 1882, the year Santa Barbara was celebrating the 100th anniversary of the Royal Presidio, three Californios, who begrudged the Americano take-over of California, held up a San Luis stage about two miles west of the Los Alamos station. Besides the Wells-Fargo box, the driver's watch was taken. It was a unique item as it was highly personalized, monogramed and containing his wife's picture. All losses were reported, but no restitution was made to the driver, personal property was not insured.

> A Californio referred to a Spanish-speaking, Catholic person of Latin American descent born in Alta California between 1769 and 1848. Alta California is the area that roughly corresponds to modern-day California.

Hudson's Saloon in Guadalupe had the onerous occasion to serve a group of Mexican vaqueros from the Jesus Maria Ranch (Ontiveros homestead). Liquored up on tequila, they became so disorderly and belligerent that they were bounced out of the barroom. Hudson received a stab wound for his efforts to eject the men. This enraged other elements of Guadalupe for Hudson was a popular bartender. A vigilante mob formed on the spot. Armed with hickory wagon spokes, neck yokes and blacksmith tools from the Hart Brothers wheelwright shop, the men pursued the drunken rabble.

While the inebriated scoundrels scrambled to get into their saddles and leave, they soon found themselves beaten, bruised and facing a lynching at the nearest telegraph pole. In the melee, the youngest drunk had fall from his hip pocket an object which drew much attention. It was the stagecoach driver's hunting-case watch, so identified by his monogram and his wife's photograph! Cooler heads prevailed and law enforcement was called.

It was later established the watch was won in a game of Monte from an unidentified stranger. Had the vigilantes had their way, his innocence would not have had the time to be established. The young vaquero had an alibi for his whereabouts the night of the stage robbery near Los Alamos and was released from legal custody and the whole to-do over the stabbing passed away as Hudson recovered from his wound.

Michael Mullee

Christmas night of 1881 brought a somewhat dubious fellow to Santa Maria. He was small with a red mustache so long it could almost be tied beneath his chin. He was described as "having a puckish bulldog face." He first introduced himself as Michael Mullee but his nickname was "Tambo." He hailed from the Barbary Coast.

He was the enterprising sort and in short order became a nuisance in Santa Maria. His business was of the lowest order and attracted those with the character to match. Brawls and disputes broke out wherever he was doing business. He catered to man's worst inclinations and before long a committee of vigilantes formed against him. Mullee was given forty-eight hours to leave town "or else." Mullee tried facing the angry mob with a constable at his side. Technically, Mullee was breaking no laws, but he was a magnet for the unsavory. The constable took one look at the angry group and determined to take the night off.

A bonfire was built at Broadway and Main Streets. Tar and feathers were procured and prepared. Mullee was nothing if not a good judge of human nature. From his first night in Santa Maria, he understood how people saw and perceived him. He could read the temperature in a room. Wisely, having prepared for this eventuality, Mullee managed the mob. He definitely preferred the humiliation of tar and feathers to the noose.

> **Tarring and feathering** is a form of public torture and punishment used to enforce unofficial justice. It was used on the early American frontier, mostly as a type of mob vengeance.

October 13, 1882, just passed midnight, Mullee rode the pole shouldered by two men toward the river and the county line. Smeared with tar and covered in feathers, his all but naked body shook with cold and fright. As they approached the edge of town, a circus troupe traveling in four or five large wagons, pulled out of the road to allow the grisly procession the right of way. As the troupers poked their heads out to see the sight, Mullee called out though chattering teeth, "Hey want to buy an Ostridge?"

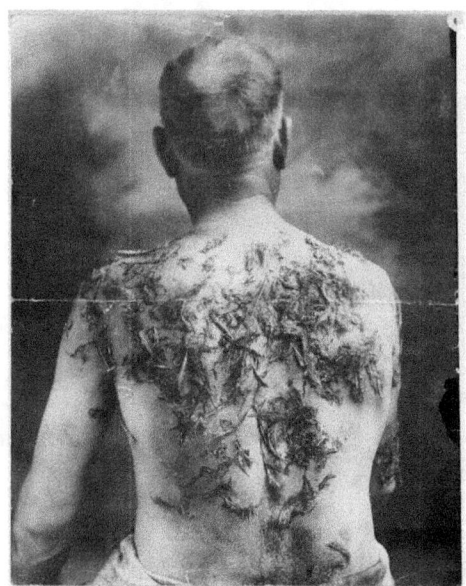

Despite his proclivity for attracting the worst of humanity, he engendered with his humor enough sympathy in this vigilante mob to crush their anger. Ultimately, they returned his clothes and told him he could walk the rest of the way out of town under his own power, and at the river they would give him his saddle horse.

Mullee wrangled his way into his clothes, the tar and feathers quite firmly affixed, and crossed the county line at the Santa Maria River. Mullee bid them farewell with a fair amount of bravado and suggested, "I hope, next time, we'll meet under more auspicious circumstances."

The commotion created at Broadway and Main Streets had created enough clamor to raise awareness of a few other disreputable characters that the residents of Santa Maria were in no mood for to tolerate vagrancy or allergies to work. *The Santa Maria Times* reported that the railroad did a brisk business the next day as associates and kindred spirits of "Tambo" Michael Mullee made their way out of town on the rail.

Not much was heard from Mullee after his tar and feathering, but he didn't go far. In this June, 1883, article from the *Los Angeles Times* we can see, he was always working an angle, just NOT in Santa Maria. Charges were later dismissed.

> **Charged with Robbery.**
> Michael Mullee was up before Judge Morgan yesterday, charged with robbery. It seems he inveigled a Mexican into Spanishtown and persuaded him to bet $10 on his ability to sing a Spanish song. The bets, in the shape of a $20-piece, were put behind the bar, when a dispute arose and the complaining witness demanded back his $10; but about that time Mullee got hold of the $20 and ran away. Some of the bystanders accommodated him by holding the Mexican so that he could not pursue. He complained to the police, however, and Mr. Mullee was caught. At last accounts he was looking for $500 bail.

The Santa Maria Vigilantes

"I joined with blood," admitted Orlando Wood Maulsby in his published 1931 autobiography Rolling Stone. O. W. Maulsby was born October 5, 1856, in Wayne County, Indiana.

Arriving in Santa Maria during a severe draught was less than an encouraging start for O.W., his wife and baby. His timing couldn't have been worse. There hadn't been a single drop of rain through the winter and many settlers were so extremely discouraged they were packing out even as the Maulsbys were arriving. A new strategy was needed. So O.W. determined to settle his wife, Melinda Beeson Maulsby, and his baby girl, Lulu Armenta, with relatives and go to the northern part of the state to look for employment.

Melinda and O.W. Maulsby

He purchased a stage ticket and prepared to leave the following morning. In the night, a deluge of rain fell raising the Santa Ynez River so high that the stage could not get across. He traded his stage ticket for a steamer ticket but had to wait for a boat. The rain continued and the railroad bridge across the Santa Maria River went out so he couldn't reach the steamer landing.

Santa Maria wouldn't let Maulsby leave! The rain had changed everyone's outlook. Farmers began plowing and seeding the land. Merchants were sending rush orders by telegraph for heavy supplies.

Landing a job as a station agent, Maulsby was greeted by Mr. Cook, the liveryman. Face-to-face, man-to-man Cook asked Maulsby, "Well, are you with us or agin' us?" Maulsby initially thought the reference was to staying in the valley.

Cook told Maulsby to come down to his stable that night at 10 o'clock and get signed up. Santa Maria had found itself recently invaded by a band of gunmen and general bad actors. Law was not being enforced. It was seventy-five miles over the San Marcos Pass to Santa Barbara, the county seat, ninety miles via Gaviota Pass and one hundred and forty miles via the coast route to reach sworn officers of the law with details and evidence of a criminal nature. These were only wagon roads and communication was slow. Santa Maria was like an island, isolated from law enforcement and feeling threatened. It was becoming a favorite resort for those who made their business slugging, drugging and robbing travelers. They even found Santa Maria a great haven to rest up and heal up with excellent medical care readily available thanks to Doc Lucas.

Maulsby learned at his first meeting that night about a group of outlaws known as the Bad Fourteen. They had decided to make Santa Maria their headquarters. Maulsby received a speedy induction into the vigilantes. Cook presented a sheet of foolscap paper on which was written a preamble, an oath and a penalty. After a brief reading, Maulsby agreed to sign. John Tunnell and Barny Devine approached: one grabbed his hand, the other rolled back his sleeve and, with a sack needle, drew a penful of blood. O.W. Maulsby signed the foolscap with his own blood and thereby became a full-fledged member of the Santa Maria Vigilantes.

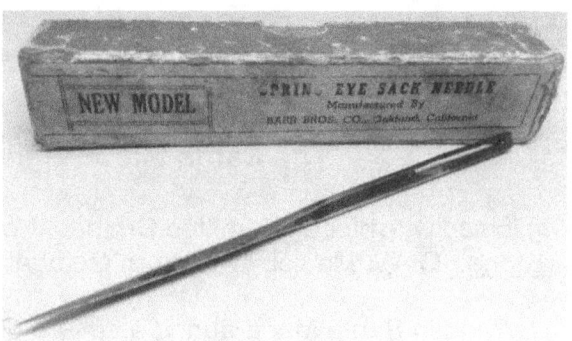

Sack Needle

It was very shortly after that the vigilantes of Cook's stable took secret charge of the execution of E.L. Criswell. In his autobiography, Maulsby makes special note that it is the law-abiding citizens, men of good character, that have made decisions for Santa Maria. While we are named vigilantes, we are "the better element of the population."

The Santa Barbara law enforcement agencies didn't agree. A lynching was not to their liking. News of the after dark activities of the vigilantes had reached the county seat. The sheriff, on hearing some details, wrote a letter to the justice of the peace at Santa Maria demanding a coroner's jury investigation and report. On one such occasion, the justice of the peace wrote back stating "...the jury, after a full and complete investigation, found him guilty of being dead. Signed, Justice of the Peace."

The vigilantes were armed, and their justice was often with a rope, but the bandits were equally armed. Their crimes, large and small, often resulted in death or maiming. Every man had a knife and a gun. Some were better at using them than others.

Small Arms of the 1800s

The Industrial Revolution led many to an improved way of life. It led others to an even more impoverished existence of living hand-to-mouth in squalid quarters. This revolution was the transformation of society, introducing new manufacturing processes in Europe and the United States, dating from between 1760 to about 1840. The development of trade and the rise of business (some might refer to this as capitalism) were among the major causes of the Industrial Revolution. Goods that had once been painstakingly crafted by hand started to be produced in mass quantities by machines in factories thanks to the introduction of new machines and techniques. One industry which prospered enormously was the manufacture of fire arms. The Industrial Revolution birthed all new manufacturing processes concerning gunsmithing and cartridge ammunition.

Weapons that were used during the 1600 until early 1800 were mostly muskets, rifles, pistols, and swords. Muskets were used by infantry men, rifles by hunters, and pistols and swords by high-ranking officers. Muskets were slow and difficult to load. Depending on the man, it took about 30 seconds to load a musket. Change was coming to the new frontier. Talented machinists fabricated purpose-built machinery to manufacture guns. Talented gunsmiths built guns from scratch.

The Rifle

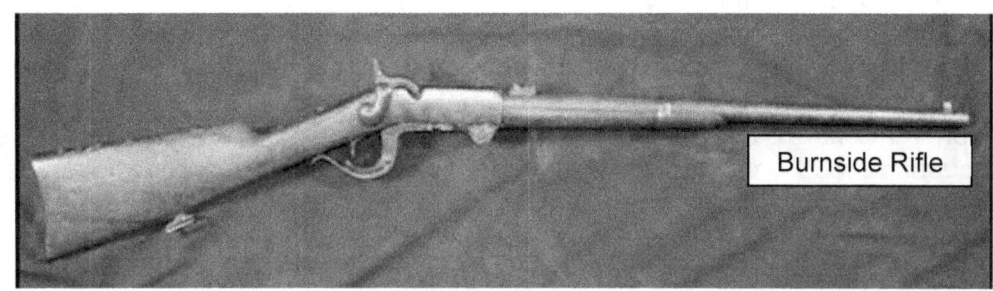

Burnside Rifle

Commonly used rifles in the early 1850s were smooth-bore, muzzle loading, cap-and-ball muskets and long-barreled rifles (AKA Kentucky or Pennsylvania rifle). Rifles were long, heavy, and slower to reload between shots than a musket. The advantage was that they could be very accurate at long range in the hands of a marksman, outlaw or lawman.

In the mid-1850s, with the advent of the metallic cartridge, single shot, breach loading rifles, known as the Burnside and the Sharps, started to make their mark. Loading was faster, and they eliminated the need to carry gun powder, primers and bullets separately. No more worries about wet gunpowder. These rifles were large caliber, heavy and very accurate.

In quick step came the repeating rifle, Henry and Winchester being the most famous. The most common type was the lever action: a number of cartridges were loaded into a cylinder under the barrel and a lever was used to load the chamber then used again to eject the fired shell and reload. These rifles were a bit shorter and lighter than earlier rifles and, with the new actions, incredibly faster.

In these days most homes would have had a shotgun for hunting and home protection. Shotguns were prominent for private business and law enforcement. There were dozens of manufacturers, but Parker made "coach" guns for Wells-Fargo; along with Winchester and Remington, these were top of the line.

Outlaw and lawman had the same weapon. Many coach and other robberies were committed with the classic double-barrel shotgun.

A third class of person also carried these weapons: in addition to the outlaws and lawmen were the vigilantes. They carried a variety of pistols, too. In the early 1850s, these were single shot cap-and-ball guns. Many were so large they were carried in holsters attached to the horse's saddle instead of their waist.

The Revolver

Samuel Colt, an American inventor and industrialist from Hartford, Connecticut, was born on July 19, 1814 and died on January 10, 1862. He patented the revolver on February 25, 1836. He died one of the wealthiest men in America. He made the mass production of revolvers commercially viable.

During the Seminole War, Captain Samuel Walker of the Texas Rangers had obtained some of the first Colt revolvers produced and saw first-hand their effective use as his 15-man unit crushed a larger force of 70 Comanches in Texas. Walker wanted to order Colt revolvers for use by the Rangers in the Mexican–American War. He traveled to New York City in search of Colt. He met Colt in a gunsmith's shop on January 4, 1847, and ordered 1,000 revolvers. Walker suggested a few changes; the new revolvers would have to hold six shots instead of five, have enough firepower to kill either a human or a horse with a single shot and be quicker to reload. This large order allowed Colt to establish a new firearms business. Colt hired Eli Whitney Blake, who was established in the arms business, to make his guns. Colt used his prototype and Walker's improvements as the basis for a new design. From this new design, Blake produced the first thousand-piece order known as the Colt Walker. The company then received an order for a thousand more. Colt shared the profits at $10 per pistol for both orders.

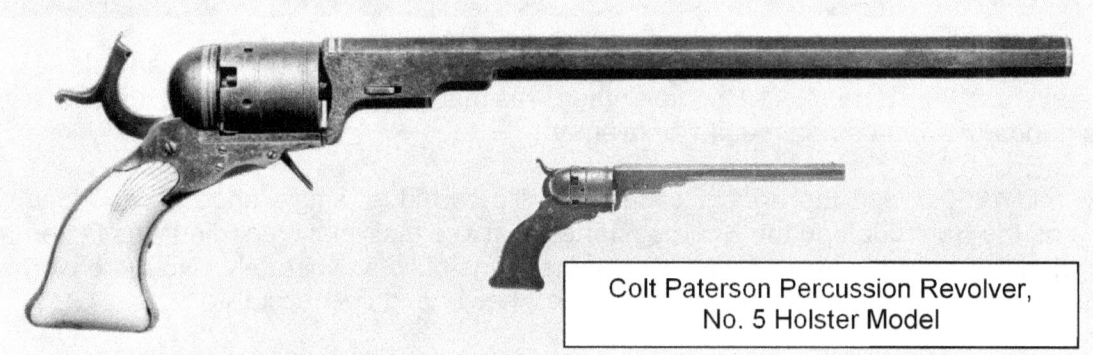

Colt Paterson Percussion Revolver, No. 5 Holster Model

Colt firearms were used widely during the settling of the western frontier. Colt's revolvers were employed as a sidearm by both civilians and soldiers. A revolver which could fire six times without reloading helped soldiers and settlers fend off larger forces which were not armed in the same way. Colt's manufacturing methods were sophisticated for their time, and his use of interchangeable parts helped him become one of the first to use the assembly line efficiently. Add to a good product the innovative use of art, celebrity endorsement, and corporate gifting to promote his merchandise and Colt is a pioneer in advertising, product placement, and mass marketing. It was said, "God created men, and Sam Colt made them equal."

Lynching in Santa Maria

The difference between lynching and hanging is that lynching is the execution of a person by mob action without due process of law, while hanging is the act of suspending a person by the neck in order to execute that person according to law. The term "lynching" is derived from the name of Charles Lynch (1736–96), a Virginia planter and justice of the peace who, during the American Revolution, headed an irregular court formed to punish loyalists.

Edmund Luther Criswell

May 12, 1890, was the culmination of a lifetime of unfortunate choices for Edmund Luther Criswell. Masked men entered the back of his saloon and executed him, a man in protective custody. Vigilantes had been maintaining order in central coast communities since the 1850s. The sparsity of lawmen at the ready to handle crime in a timely manner had given rise to groups taking matters into their own hands. Routinely, western towns posted warnings to the lawless, and Santa Maria was no exception to making intentions clear. If words weren't enough, certainly the actions of their "Citizens' Committee" were. Leading the committee in Santa Maria were R. D. Cook and Henry Stowell.

Criswell came to the Central Coast on the same trails and rails as others of his timeline. Leaving reconstruction and a dubious military record behind, Criswell showed himself as a business man with a trade. He took ads in the *Santa Maria Times* promoting his skills. He worked on several large town projects including the Jones and Son rebuild on Broadway.

Notice Warning Undesirables to Leave Town

PUBLIC NOTICE

The undersigned are hereby notified to leave this town of Santa Maria on or before Sunday morning the 28th inst., at 9 o'clock, as you show no means of earning a legitimate livelihood. In event of not complying with the above you will be deal with accordingly.

**E. Potter,
Geo. Crawford,
John Doe Drapper,
Worth Brown,
Dick Duke
and Others.**

By order of
CITIZENS' COMMITTEE.
Santa Maria, Sept. 26th, 1884.

Raising from the Ashes.

Almost before the ashes had cooled Jones & Son had commenced removing the debris and collecting the material for their new building, which is to be of brick, two stories high. This week Mr. Criswell has finished the brick foundation, which shows that the new structure will have a frontage of 51 feet on Broadway by a depth of fifty feet. The plans have not been fully drawn yet as Jones & Son are waiting until after the meeting of the Masonic Lodge this evening, which order is desirous of joining them in putting up the building.

In the end, Criswell is summed up by a despicable action he couldn't walk back. The story is oft-told and with some discrepancies. The only non-disputed fact is that Criswell was not mourned in the Santa Maria Valley.

**E. L. Criswell,
PLASTERER.
Lathing, Plastering, Bricklaying.**

Special attention given to country work

The Criswell story is really by definition a lynching. That term would have offended the sensibilities of the citizens of that day, so from their lips to our history books, by conventional wisdom it is well accepted that Santa Maria has had only one "hanging."

Madison "Matt" Jessee, a deputy constable under the direction of Constable Isaac Wesley "Doc" Southard, recalls events in an interview in the *Santa Maria Times* published in May 1932. Jessee was about 31 at the time of the incident and recalls it for the *Times* at age 73.

"As near as I can remember, it was back in '85 (actually it was May 12, 1890) when Criswell paid with his life for the killing of

Constable 'Doc' Southard under whom I was constable," Jessee said. "Criswell ran a saloon and general hangout in the middle of the first block down from Broadway. In front of his place, he had a blackboard upon which he began to post objectionable notices about the love affair of a dressmaker with a local citizen. (Could this be the lovely Miss Hourihan and Mr. Ulysses Grant Battles?) The latter complained to Southard, who warned Criswell not to repeat the offense.

"Criswell, a strapping big fellow and apparently fearless, continued to use his blackboard in the same manner. Southard upon being told again, went to see Criswell who was in front of his place of business. Southard in no uncertain terms told him 'to cut it out.'"

Jessee quoted Criswell as saying, "I'll write all I want to, and you can't stop me."

Continuing his story, Jessee said, "Criswell started in his place of business saying that Southard wouldn't talk that way to an armed man."

A Murderous Attack.

On Monday last a murderous affray occurred at Los Alamos in which E. L. Criswell and son of this place were principals. It appears that young Criswell went into a saloon with another young man to get a glass of beer and his father who was sitting near ordered the barkeeper not to give it to them. The beer was drawn and placed before them notwithstanding, and Criswell became highly enraged and siezed a mallet and struck his son on the forehead. The boy ran out and his father pursued him until he was captured and placed under arrest. His examination commenced on Thursday and the trial was still in progress at our latest advices yesterday. Cooper and Cothran were for the defense and Cooper had already been fined twice for contempt of Court and Cothran only escaped the same fate by the skin of his teeth.

It was next reported that a shot rang out! Criswell had a pistol hidden on him and fired first with Southard drawing and firing immediately afterwards. Both men fell.

Southard was mortally wounded and Criswell seriously. Dr. William Thomas Lucas was called. Jessee placed a pillow beneath Southard's head where he had fallen, apparently shot through the heart. Both men were examined, Criswell was shot through the breast bone, the bullet passing through to the back just under the skin where Doc Lucas cut it out.

Criswell received expert medical treatment and was expected to survive. Guards were assigned to provide supervised custody for Criswell in his residence at the back of his 76 Saloon. There had been rumblings in town all during the day as it became obvious that he would live. The guards had been placed as much for his protection as to ensure he was available to face justice in a Santa Barbara court.

Criswell suffered severely as much because of his terrible reputation as by his regrettable actions. It had been suggested that Criswell was a Union deserter. Further tarnishing him was his attack on his own son. In today's court, such prejudicial information would not have been allowed for consideration, but a vigilante mob doesn't "unknow" its own discriminations or biases when they make their verdict.

Matt Jessee, served as deputy constable in 1886, long before Santa Maria was incorporated.

During the night, a number of masked men entered the saloon and proceeding to the little room in the back, which was Criswell's bedroom, disarmed the guards, bound Criswell's hands and feet, threw a rope over the rafter and hung him until he suffocated to death.

The body of Criswell was buried on a Monday afternoon around 4 o'clock in the Santa Maria Cemetery. No headstone was ever placed. It remains unmarked to this day.

An inquest is a judicial inquiry in common law jurisdictions, particularly one held to determine the cause of a person's death. Conducted by a judge, jury, or government official, an inquest may or may not require an autopsy carried out by a coroner or medical examiner. They determine the identity of the deceased and cause of death. They classify the manner of death as natural, accidental, homicide, suicide, or undetermined.

There was an inquest to review the incident of this vigilante justice. The jury was composed of W.T. Morris, R.D. Cook, George C. Smith, W.T. Dutton, George R. Tunnell, R.D. Hill, J.D. Grady, J.R. Weeks and Horatio L. Nelson. They pronounced their profound concerns that even with so despicable a character as obviously was E.L. Criswell, a lynching reflects badly upon the citizenry.

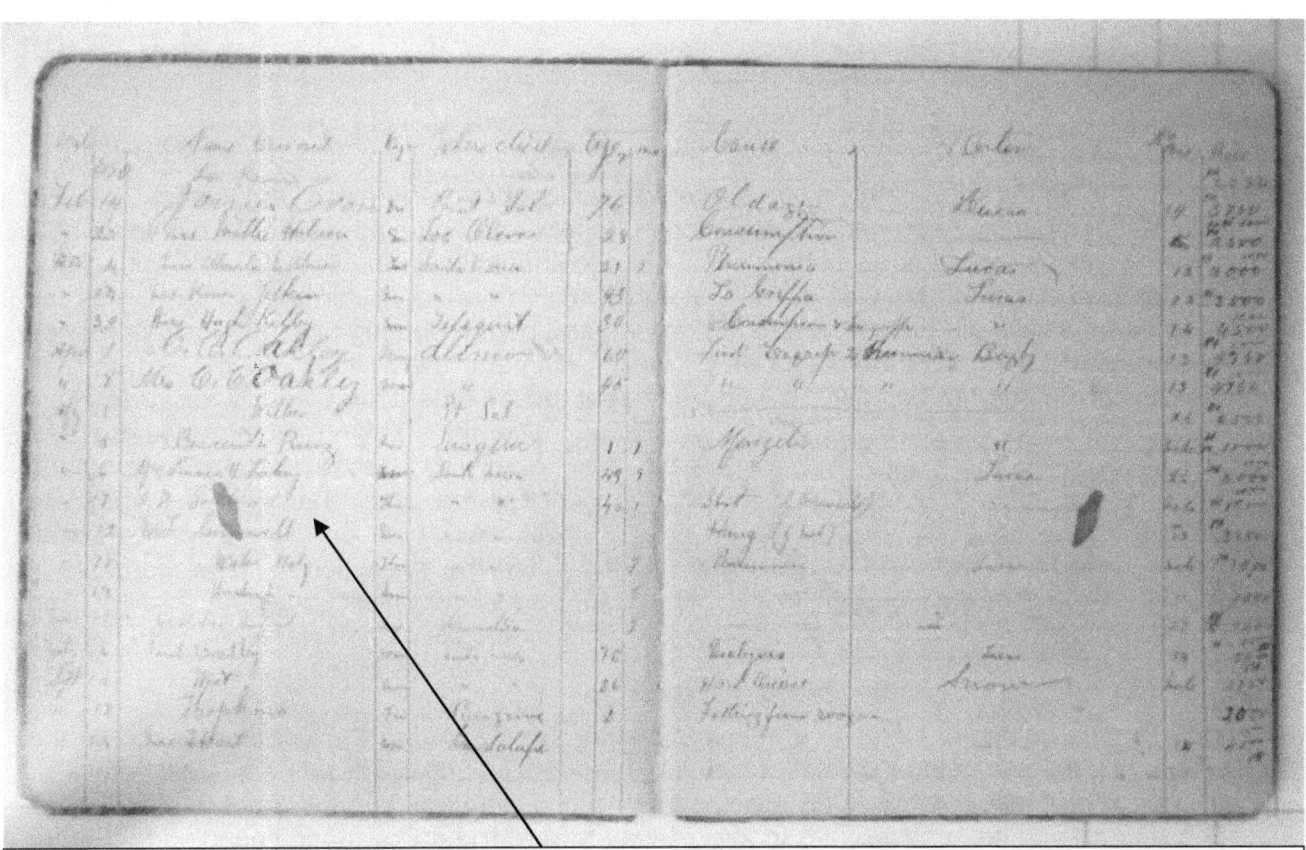

Mortality log book for Santa Maria. Southard is listed on the 7th as "shot." Criswell follows on the 12th as "hung."

Trinidad German

There is plenty of criticism for vigilante justice but, as was the case of one Trinidad German, the law wasn't protecting society. When German was 24, he rode up to the door of a crippled Indian named Lanterio and said, "You have lived long enough." and then killed him. He continued his murder spree finding another man and shooting him twice without a word of warning. He persisted in robbing stagecoaches and killing indiscriminately. Reportedly on the loose near Los Alamos, the well-known murderer when captured was found guilty of second-degree murder. He was surprising pardoned for $1,000 gift fourteen years into his life sentence. Unfortunately, German was not of a reformed character.

Forensics of a Legal Hanging

Date: 31 January 1891. Mark Fleisher, a prominent general merchant store operator and other Santa Maria citizens attended Sheriff Broughton's "necktie party" in Santa Barbara. It was an official execution of Ramon Lopez for the murder of Mary Dezirelli.

From California newspapers c. 1886.

Lopez shot the young woman three times after she refused to marry him. On October 20,1890, a highly respectable lady spurned the affections of an ex-con and was murdered by him in cold blood the headlines read. Lopez made a small effort to shoot himself putting his pistol to his head but then missed the shot! He was quickly taken by law enforcement, fortunately for him as the father of the now slain girl pushed him to the ground and began beating him. On-lookers rushed toward the scene and had there been less law enforcement, there would have been no trial. Lopez was known and not popular. He had been sent to San Quentin previously for three years after the stabbing death of a young local man. Witnesses from Santa Maria reported the hanging a complete success both on the part of the sheriff and the executioner. The murderer, it was reported, yielded coolly and gracefully to his fate of death for his treacherous crime.

The press made quite a declaration of the whole affair. At 10 o'clock the Sheriff dressed for the execution, putting on a neat black suit of clothing, black socks and black slippers. Just before 11 o'clock, the sheriff told Lopez that his time had come and read the death warrant to him. Lopez clasped a crucifix to his breast as he made his way toward the gallows accompanied by Father Caballeria in full canonicals, reading a prayer. Lopez was reported as pale but composed as he mounted the gallows steps without assistance and took a position over the middle drop. Ignoring the crowd, Lopez remained calm. Father Caballeria stepped forward to address the people of the city of Santa Barbara telling them Ramon Lopez's last statements. Father Caballeria reported that this morning the condemned wished for those present to be told that he acknowledges his guilt and asks forgiveness. Additionally, he asks pardon of all those he has offended and pardons all those who have offended him in this life. He bids his friends good-bye and asks for prayer. Lopez turned his face briefly toward the sun and shook hands with Sheriff Broughton as Father Caballeria finished his part in the grim business. Lopez' arms and feet bound with heavy black cords, Sheriff Broughton put the black cap on him while Deputy Sheriff Wheeler adjusted the noose.

Death followed instantaneously at 11:04. Sheriff Broughton signaled with his handkerchief, the spring was touched, the heavy trap door swung free and Ramon Lopez was dispatched into eternity for his unlawful ways. His body dropped heavily with a fall of 6.5 feet. His neck was broken and death was painless. The crowd stood quiet and motionless, one man fainted at the spectacle and had to be revived. Justice was served.

Above, Criswell's rope had been cut and tied for a short drop, meaning he was to die by strangulation and not as a result of a broken neck which was quick and painless. Slow drop could mean 3-5 minutes of "dancing at the end of a rope."

Gunfights of the West

Actual gunfights in the Old West were rare. When they did occur, the cause for each varied widely. Some were simply the result of heated emotions, while others were longstanding feuds or between bandits and lawmen at a single point in time. Gunslingers or gunfighters were individuals in the American Old West who gained a reputation of being dangerous with a gun and participated in gunfights and shootouts. Today, the term "gunslinger" is often used to denote someone who is quick on the draw with a pistol.

The gunfighter could be a lawman, outlaw, cowboy, or shooting exhibitionist, but was generally a hired gun who made a living with his weapons. He was hired when local law enforcement failed or was absent, and he led the vigilante members or his own deputized individuals in "citizen committees" in pursuing accused muckrakers or known criminals. He helped them quiet their communities and restore order to their streets. Sometimes just pushing them on to the next town was enough to satisfy his contract with citizens and city officials. Asking these elements to be gone by sundown was common. The danger for all was when the order was ignored and trouble roiled to the surface. In other instances, the gunfighter might be hired by someone who wanted to bully a community into submissive behavior. Even in the 1800s, "private security" could keep law enforcement turning a blind eye. Some of the well-known gunslingers were Bill Hickok, Billy the Kid, Jessee James, Wyatt Earp, John Wesley Hardin and Bat Masterson.

Miller-Stokes Duel

Is it a duel or a family feud? In March 1914, Joe Miller and Braulio Stokes settled a score in a lonely shack off West Main Street near the Pacific Coast Railway Depot. The two engaged in a "shootout" with pistols resulting in the death of Stokes and the near fatal wounding of Miller. Miller was shot through-and-through by one of the bullets from Stokes' revolver. Five shots in total were fired arousing neighbors and night watchman Matt Jessee. All parties were taken into custody.

Bartholomew William Barclay "Bat" Masterson was on born November 26, 1853, and died on October 25, 1921. Bat was a U.S. Army scout, lawman, professional journalist and known for his exploits in the 19th and early 20th-century American Old West.

PISTOL SHOTS SETTLE FUED

The inquest was held Tuesday afternoon. Witnesses testified that Stokes started the row. He had also stolen a pistol form the Saint James Stable where he was employed. Witnesses were Matt Jessee, G.L. Blosser, H.H. Bardin and Dr. O.P. Paulding. The verdict of the jury was that Stokes came to his death by gunshot wounds at the hands of Joe Miller. The two were in conflict over a woman, Mrs. Minnie Trejo, who was estranged from her husband and had a boy age five.

Santa Maria was slow to give up its vigilante ways. As late at 1936, there were those who believed they could make their own rules and enforce them as evidenced by this letter on hand now archived at the Santa Maria Valley Historical Society.

                                    Santa Maria, Calif.
                                    Oct. 19, 1936

Mr. Bates, Foreman
Betteravia, Calif.

Dear Sir:

   The committe of our organization has turned in a very unsatisfactory report as to the labor situation in the sugar factory.

   "We find after a through investigation of the matter that Mr. Bates doesn't follow the American triditions of fair play and justice in employing his help. There is a evidence of a great majority of colored men and a small minority of white employees.

   We recomend that Mr. Bates be notified at once and consider that situation in our own light. We will tolerate twenty percent of his choice; but we demand that eighty per cent shall be of our choosing. Mr. Bates, we demand that eighty percent shall be white men employed in your department.

   With in five day of mailing this letter if Mr. Bates doesn't consider this chang inaperation and make the changes there by eliminating the dark element form his employment a second copy of this letter will be sent to the President of the Union Sugar Company. If this does not releive the unfairness of employment in your department we will take dastrict measures we will take the matter up with the members of the organization which total 89,000 members in California."

   Mr. Bates, we consider you a man of good inteligence and reasoning power therefore we know that you will adhere to this warning. In fact it would be very advisable if you would use a little logic and make the changes in your department.

                           Yours with Honor

                           Knights of the Vigilantes

Chapter 814
H/E.L.J.

Chapter 2: Child Murder and Child Murderers

In any scenario, the death of a child is among the most devastating. Pedicide, child murder, or child homicide is the slaying of an individual who is a minor. Our sympathies are heightened when the victim is a young child or juvenile. Thus, the deaths of minors raise public concerns. There is an inferred innocence attached to childhood. Even the most callous among society can't find a mitigation for child murder.

Every formation of the human community, even prisons, have a structure of social politics. There exists a hierarchy among all animal kingdoms. From the neutered male cat to the fertile female, a structure of significance determines everything from who eats first to which are unworthy to live or breed.

In nearly 61% of cases, it is the parent or a close family member who kills a child. It's what makes investigating crimes against children so difficult. The unimaginable has happened, and it's someone close to home in the majority of cases. When a case goes unsolved, there is a stain that, in many situations, unrightfully clings to the family or to one member.

Solomon Hill Sniper: Michael Andrew Clark, 16

With daylight is breaking on the beautiful Central Coast morning of April 25, 1965, a crew-cut, sallow-faced teen was sitting on the Solomon Pass grade watching travelers on Highway 101 some 200 yards below his perch. He had wrecked his mother's 1960 Cadillac against a guard rail. He misjudged a curve in the straining early morning light. The darkness had broken. A car came driving southbound. Michael Andrew Clark, 16, would become a killer before the sun's zenith. The shooter was wearing glasses and leather gloves. His finger found the trigger of the rifle. The rifle rose to position, and he took aim through the Weaver four-power sighted scope. He aimed for the unsuspecting driver, 18-year-old Stanley I. Manning. It was 6 a.m. He missed; his aim was too low. The bullet glanced off the right fender. The Corvette Stingray sped off toward Los Alamos to alert authorities. The first one had escaped.

Michael Andrew Clark, 16-year-old runaway from Long Beach

Clark pushed more shells into the magazine until the gun could not hold any more. The shells were reported to be armor piercing, 6.5-millimeter cartridges. Clark watched the highway. A car stopped just off the northbound lane. Taking aim, he pulled the trigger. This time, he didn't miss; the bullet pierced the man in the driver's seat. He fired again blowing out the back windshield. That bullet hit 5-year-old Kevin Reida lodging in his brain. The boy would die of his wounds. The bullet's metal jacket exploded sending steel fragments into the skull of three-year-old Kim, the

CHARLES HOGAN

little brother. The shattered glass slices the mother, Mrs. Lucille Reida. A Sunday drive had turned deadly. Kellyann, in the back seat, clamors out holding her infant sister, Karen Sue, and hides.

Lucille, blood streaming from her face, leapt from the car and ran onto the highway to try to stop another car in an attempt to get help for her family. A light colored Chevelle pulls up. Clark took aim at the driver's window. His shot flared wide right striking the rear window; which shattered but did not break. Charles C. Hogan, a Hancock student, 21 was dead. The bullet coursed through his upper body killing him all but instantly. He was a passenger in Kathleen Smith's car.

Clark watched as the frantic woman recoiled and ran up the road to the north. His eyes left her as he scrutinized a maroon Corvair that was turning onto the grassy median separating the north and south bound lanes. He placed the driver in his scope and pulled the trigger. The driver slumped over the steering wheel, and the car rolled to a stop. Joel W. Kocab sat dead in his seat with a bullet to the back of his head.

Another car approached, Clark aimed and fired; mercifully the gun is empty. He scrambled to reload and take aim. The bullet hit the car window. The driver sped away, but a girl was shot in the arm. Shattering glass wounded everyone in the vehicle.

In just 12 minutes, Clark had killed two men and a five-year-old boy. He had critically injured another child and inflicted serious wounds on numerous others. He continued to rain bullets down as cars and trucks paused to consider rendering assistance before fleeing toward Santa Maria to warn authorities. In a few minutes a black-and-white police car pulled up. The officers jump out, and the game on.

Santa Barbara County Sheriff Detective William Steele kneels over Clark's body.

Crouched behind the patrol car, officers stay low as a bullet pierced the right front fender hitting the tire and flattening it. The policemen were armed with pistols. They didn't have the fire power to reach Clark, and he knew it. Another police car joined; this officer had a "big gun." Bert Schuermann was almost immediately shot in the left forearm. Good news: more police followed him and they had big guns too.

All havoc broke loose as Clark rained bullets down on the officers as they worked their way toward him and his victims. Clark was finally taking some heat. Perhaps panic had set in or maybe he was just not prepared to face the consequences of his actions, but Clark retreated with his rifle, and, with his right hand on the barrel, he turned it toward his face. He raised up in a crouch in order to reach down with his left hand and push the trigger with his left thumb. The round ripped through his brain taking half his face and killing him instantly. The killing is over, but the case was just beginning.

Aftermath of the Shooting

Why would a mild-mannered, average, all-American boy become a berserk killer? The "why" would consume his parents for the rest of their natural days. They would face national scrutiny and a major law suit of 4.6 million dollars. The Clark family was 'well to do." Clark owned his own manufacturing company in Long Beach. Mrs. Clark was an elementary school teacher. They had two other children: a 15-year-old boy and a 10-year-old girl. Everyone was looking to them for an explanation of what possessed Michael to kill total strangers and himself and emotionally destroy his own family.

The Reida family had suffered the loss of a child, but William Reida, although surviving, was suffering from complications of his wounds. Lucille Reida nearly lost an eye and faced more surgeries. It was the trauma that their surviving children feel every day that consumed these parents.

In December 1965, William and Lucille Reida brought a wrongful death lawsuit against Forrest and Joyce Clark and Michael's Trust Fund. The suit claimed that the Clarks, Michael's parents, were negligent and culpable in the shooting rampage and that any reasonable person could have anticipated his behavior. It was stated that the parents "encouraged" the use of the Swedish Mauser, the weapon used to assassinate Kevin Reida, as a big part of his recreational time. It was further contended that the weapon was made an important part of his juvenile life-style. It was also alleged that both parents were aware of antisocial, psychotic behaviors and knew their son was likely to harm others. Knowing these things, the suit pursued that despite this understanding, they nurtured his aberrant fascination with deadly weapons.

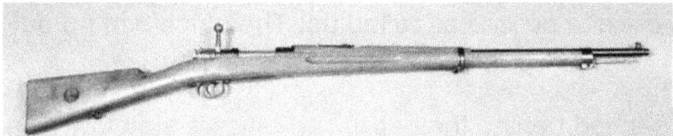

One of the accusations against the father was that he had "endeared" the murder weapon to young Clark. It was a highly customized, 6.5 X 55 mm bolt-action rifle.

The original design was by Mauser for the Nordic countries of Sweden, Norway and Demark and goes back to 1896. It's a good game rifle suitable for deer.

The location of the shooter was at an elevation of 1,052 feet. He was aiming at moving cars at an elevation of approximately 928 feet, a drop of 128 feet at a distance of .2 miles or 354 yards as the crow flies. His target could be estimated to be moving at a speed of 60-65 miles per hour. Shooting downhill a quarter mile at a fast-moving target was quite the feat.

Scene of Sudden, Tragic Death

A View From The Solomon Pass Hills

The body of Michael Clark is stretched out face down where he died Sunday after putting a bullet through his own head. This shows view Clark commanded from his sniper's position overlooking the freeway. CHP officer John Hill stands at left with rifle he was using in a futile attempt to stop Clark's barrage. The letters on photo show (A) Clark's car where he crashed it into a guard rail on an off-road curve, (B) Mrs. Kathy Smith's car in which Charles Hogan was passenger killed by Clark's shot and (C) the car of Joel Kocab, who was also killed by Clark when he stopped to give aid to the Reida family, as did Mrs. Smith. Cars in foreground were targets for Clark during ensuing gun battle with police force of about 25 men.

--Times Photo by Jim Squires

The type of bullet that was used was described as "steel clad" or "armor piercing." This may have been an error or misnomer. The amount was described as a "bag of ammo." It was claimed Clark filled his pockets with ammunition. These descriptions suggest that Clark had bulk military ammunition and not commercial hunting rounds. Military ball ammo has a hard lead core surrounded by a copper or brass coating is referred to as FMJ, full metal jacket. The purpose of the copper coating is to allow it to expand to the lands and grooves in the rifle barrel as it moves from the breech to the muzzle, imparting a spin on the bullet. Spin gives it accuracy.

Joyce and Forrest Clark, parents of the killer in court, May 1965.

Considering the skill that young Clark developed at the tutoring of his father, the quality of the rifle and the power of the ammunition he had on hand, there is clear intent on Michael Clark's part to impress his father and make a very dramatic statement in the process. Although it was later presented that he had been described as a paranoid schizophrenic, it seemed more likely at the time he was looking for some attention and approval from his father and he used Mauser, his father's prize possession, to do it. Clark did not pack anything in the car when he left home; he seemed to understand that it was a one-way trip. The case was first heard in April 1967. In December 1969, a judge dismissed the complaint against the Clarks. An appeals court reversed the ruling in part, stating the Reidas could sue Forrest Clark, but not his wife, on grounds of possible liability for failing to keep the military rifle out of Michael Clark's hands. Finally, in October 1972, damages were awarded. The amount never approached the nearly $5 million that was pursued. The Reidas receive $134,477. The jury determined that Mr. Clark was not liable for his son's behavior. Punitive damages were ruled out.

The court award gave William Reida $51,160.45 and Lucille Reida $68,251.65. Awards given to the children were: Kim $1,679.15, Kellyann $1,020.00 and Karen Sue, who was eight months old at the time, $22.50. The parents also received $12,343.64 for Kevin's death. The jury returned its verdict against the estate of Michael Andrew Clark. The money was a fraction of the original $4.6 million, which was sought, but it marked an end to what began on beautiful central coast Sunday, April 25, 1965.

Michael Andrew Clark was entombed in the mausoleum at Forest Lawn Memorial Park in Long Beach, California. He was 16 years old.

BILL AND LUCILLE REIDA
Parents of the slain child, Kevin Reida

Forensics Science before 1960

It is a common misconception that forensic investigation is new. In one form or another, for thousands of years forensic inquiries have been exercised to examine mysterious deaths.

In ancient times, the manner of death was naturally assumed by where and how the victim had been found. For instance, a man found in a body of water would have presumptively drowned, while a man found lying broken and bloodied along the side of a road would have naturally fallen and possibly been dragged by a horse. Objective observations were made and a conclusion drawn.

In the case of a suspicious death, the word of others against a possible murderer took precedence over any other facts, and, when all else failed, torture was readily available to procure a confession. Eye witness testimony was trump.

During the middle of the 12th Century, the Chinese were accredited with being the first to attempt to define the difference between natural death and criminal death. A book written by Sung Tz'u called *The Washing Away of Wrong* became an official text for coroners. The book recorded observations made by the author (e.g., strangulation victims could be detected by damaged cartilage in the neck (hyoid bone) and water collected in the lungs of drowning victims).

The Bow Street Runners have been called London's first professional police force. The force originally numbered six men and was founded in 1749 by magistrate Henry Fielding. In 1835, a former Bow Street Runner employed by Scotland Yard was the first documented case of law enforcement comparing bullets to catch a perpetrator. Henry Goddard noticed a flaw in a bullet that was traced back to the original bullet mold.

Unnamed Santa Maria Police Officer dusts for prints c. 1940

In 1788, the discovery that fingerprints were unique to each individual and could provide identification of a particular individual was cause for fingerprint analysis to become a major part of crime investigation. Dr. Nathaniel Grew published an illustrated anatomy book in which he claimed that "the arrangement of skin ridges is never duplicated in two persons." Henry Faulds was curious whether or not fingerprints remained the same despite efforts made to erase them. He experimented with volunteers, introducing pumice stone, sandpaper and even acids to determine if fingerprints would appear different after new skin growth. They didn't. In a paper published in the 1880, the scientific journal called *Nature*, Faulds wrote that bloody fingerprints or impressions on a variety of surfaces could be used for the scientific identification of criminals.

Fingerprinting had begun seeing routine use by more sophisticated law enforcement agencies in the early 1800s. As is usually true with innovative ideas, these new investigative techniques were resisted by law enforcement, and it would take many decades before fingerprinting would become an acceptable forensic tool for identifying criminals. Training and equipment took a long time to filter down into small town law enforcement agencies.

Professor Mathieu Orfila, an expert of medicinal chemistry at the University of Paris, became known as the Father of Toxicology in 1813 after he published *Traite de Poisons*. He is the first to be credited with attempting to use a microscope to assess blood and semen stains.

A few years later, a doctor "experimenting" with the corpses of dead soldiers in Malta discovered that body temperature dropped at regular intervals following death and could be used to determine the time of death.

Each of these alone, provides little, but together they offer a lead.

A German scientist named Christian Schonbein, was the first to observe that hemoglobin had the capacity to oxidize hydrogen peroxide thus inadvertently discovering the first test for the assumption of the presence of blood in 1863. Before his discovery, it was blood if investigators said it was blood. In the early 1900s, the field of forensic investigation achieved a major development with the discovery of Benzidine, a chemical compound used to develop a universal, presumptive test for blood. Benzidine is a manufactured chemical. In the past, large amounts of benzidine were used to produce dyes for cloth, paper, and leather. It was just prior to the Second World War that German scientist Walter Specht developed a chemical reagent called luminal, still used today, as a presumptive test for the presence of blood.

In 1888 Jack the Ripper, England's most notorious serial killer, precipitated the use of crime scene photography. As public streets were his crime pallet, picture making allowed for the extensive study of the scenes while shielding the public from the gruesome realities and clearing the streets for community use. All pictures were extensively studied in an effort to detect clues. Scotland Yard was the first to have attempted criminal profiling as a result of the Ripper's savage *modus operandi*.

Perhaps the most profound proclamation of forensic science is detailed by this emphatic statement made in 1904 by Edmond Locard, "every contact leaves a trace." Crime scene investigation still takes a human brain to rationalize and conceptualize what has happened. With a plethora of technological advancements, forensic investigative tools have made understanding a crime scene simpler than it used to be. However, despite all advancements, never is it forgotten that the human factor comes into play in every crime, and it isn't just the

investigators who are getting smarter; the criminal too is benefitting from this advanced knowledge, both in creating misinformation and in disguising himself from law enforcement.

Harry Eckland Blochman Case

Santa Maria's first child murder occurred the evening before the 4th of July 1901. Harry "Dutchy" Blochman ran out his front door at 8:30 pm to search the town for adventure. By 11:00 pm, his father began to wonder if he had been kidnapped, and on the 6th, his mutilated body was found close to home. His adoptive parents lived the nightmare of not knowing or understanding what happened to their young son in those last moments. The *why* will never be answered.

Santa Maria in the summer of 1901 had become a town! It was drawing a lively crowd for its parades and celebrations. Folks from all around the valley rode in to enjoy the festivities and gaiety of the proud city! The population had swollen from barely a 1,000 to several thousand. All were welcome! The frivolity was good for businesses, especially the bars, restaurants and hotels. People were camping in the open fields; there were no more rooms available. The atmosphere was one of revelry.

For a thirteen-year-old boy amid all of this excitement, there was much to explore. When young Harry's friends arrived on his doorstep at 801 S. Broadway to watch the parade with him, they discovered that an alarm had been sent out that he was missing since the evening before. No one remembered for certain seeing him since 8:45 pm. His parents would wait three days before the terrible truth would be known. Harry Blochman was a tender-age murder victim.

WITH HUE AND CRY THEY HUNT KELSOE

The Late Harry Blochman.

The Santa Maria boy of thirteen years, who was killed under circumstances of extreme brutality by a man who has since fled the country. Judging from the nature of his wounds, local detectives are inclined to believe that his slayer may be the man that murdered Robbie Hislop.

The San Francisco Examiner, Mon, Jul, 8, 1901

SANTA BARBARA, CAL., MONDAY AFTERNOON, JULY 8, 1901.

MYSTERY OF HARRY BLOCHMAN'S DISAPPEARANCE WAS MURDER

Body of the Boy Supposed to Have Been Kidnaped Is Found in Field Near Santa Maria---Knife and Bullet Wounds Tell the Story---Lynching Probable.

Newspapers reported that angry citizens of the county were out with guns. Two hundred men with pistols and rifles went out searching the county for William Kelso, a man of dubious reputation and the *ruffman* believed to be the murderer, under devilish horror and cruelty, of Harry Blochman. He was the focus of the investigation within moments of the discovery of young Blochman's body. "If they should find this man, woe to him," the journalist cried out. "It will go hard for the rage is such that he would be lucky if he escapes hanging to the nearest tree."

The intensity of the investigation was enthusiastic and aggressive. Some light was cast onto the nature of the crime as another young boy who was interviewed reported that Kelso tried to lure him into the bean field for 15 cents. Harry's body was recovered in that same field.

The inquest revealed all too clearly the heinous nature of the crime perpetrated. It began by reporting the death as the work of a savage brute. Harry was stabbed to death with a pocket knife "sent home with such force as to penetrate three inches." Two of the blows penetrated the skull, and one eye was all but cut out. Over the heart was a deep stab, and altogether there were nine wounds, any one of which would have proved fatal, besides numerous slighter injuries. The knife was buried to the hilt three to four inches deep in five instances. It was further noted on the indictment that Harry Blochman's body lay in the hot sun for three days and was in an advanced stage of decay. The ground in the bean field on which the body lay exposed a terrible struggle had taken place. Great splashes of blood, close to where the boy lay face down partially buried in the soft earth, revealed that he had fallen with some violence. His cap lay on the disturbed ground twenty feet from his body. The inquest jury promptly found a verdict of murder and charged William H. Kelso with the crime.

July 9th, 1901, further evidence was recovered in the bean field where the tragedy occurred. The butt-end of a whip covered with blood was unearthed further pointing to the degenerate nature of the murderer.

> I have been arrested for a crime that I certainly never committed. In fact I didn't know that any murder had been committed until I was put under arrest at the Henry stock ranch in San Luis Obispo county. I was very much surprised at the arrest. I had seen no papers of any kind and had no idea they were after me. Had I known Sheriff Stewart was after me I would have given myself up at the nearest town. I knew Harry Blochman the murdered boy slightly. I saw him on the afternoon of the 3rd of July when he stood about while I and another man were talking. I may or may not have spoken to him. In fact I only think I talked to him from hearing him described by Nat Stewart. I didn't know his name until they accused me of killing him. I certainly do not remember seeing him that night.
>
> There is a story that I offered another boy 15 cents to walk across the field where the murder was committed. I am pretty sure I didn't.
>
> I didn't understand until today what a "moral degenerate" was. I thought it meant a fellow who was "bug-housedt" or crazy. Of this charge again I am innocent. My life has been like most other men's, I've done some boozing and have run around some, but I never got into any trouble before. I think I will have no trouble in proving that I have been pretty straight. The thing now is to get out of this the best way I can. I don't know how bad it looks against me because I haven't seen the papers. I will write to my folks today and ask them what they think about my case. I've got $10 that's all. So far I don't know what I am going to do and I don't like to talk too much.
> WILL KELSO.

Walter Jackson, William Kelly, Frank Kellman or William Kelso, was a prisoner in a dark cell in the county jail. He was under arrest for the murder of Harry Blochman. He was placed in custody and incarcerated by Sheriff Nat Stewart and Deputy Garrett Blosser. Kelso was held in San Luis Obispo under feeling that an attempt to lynch the child murderer might be made by the citizenry of Santa Maria. The venue for the trial would not be Santa Maria.

Kelso was taken in overalls covered in spots which officers believed to be blood. He was 23 years old, dark complexioned, small in stature at 5 feet 4 inches, yet wiry. He had a large head, firm physique and a face that tapered toward the chin. His brown curly hair was thinning and taking him toward baldness. He wore a small mustache. His eyes were small and set close together.

Most distinguishing was that he had no teeth in his upper jaw. He was a heavy drinker and used tobacco incessantly.

False Evidence

Witnesses James Davisson and Dr. J. B. Arrellanes, dentist, attested to seeing Kelso with Blochman minutes before his murder. It was Frederick Emory Strong who asserted his wagon was stolen to precipitate Kelso's escape.

> **"DETECTIVE" LUNBECK**
>
> **Once A Friend To Harry Blochman, Now Working For The Defense**
>
> An interesting feature of the Blochman murder case has developed through the attitude of Norman P. Lunbeck, who has been an active figure in "digging up" evidence to be used at the trial.

> These are the men who will decide William Kelso's fate:
> William F. Warren, William Delkner, James Anderson, Nicholas Conrad, A. W. Potter, J. W. Robbins, Thomas Rutherford, Joseph W. Cave, Joel R. Fithian, Charles Ealand, S. P. Stow, F. M. Whitney.
> The greatest difficulty that had been experienced by the attorneys in the selection of jurors was due to the general knowledge had of the case and the formation of opinions based upon conversations and newspaper reports. There were but few who had not discussed the murder and whose minds had not been influenced by verbal and printed accounts of the developments following the commission of the crime.

> The following list of witnesses have been subpoenaed to appear before the court:
> Alfonso Arellanes, J. B. Arellanes Jr., L. E. Blochman, Ida M. Blochman, Mrs. M. Stearns, Frank Culhane, H. Steinhart, G. L. Blosser, Dan Blosser, James Davisson, Homer Hughes, Wm. Langlois, R. V. Jameson, F. Loustalot, J. P. Loustalot, L. J. Morris, Dr. Paulding, Earl Colyin, Elmer Trainer, Geo. Howard, M. Howard, Geo. Black, Ed Williams, J. H. Strong, Fred Strong, Leslie Knotts, Miss Bessie Morris, William Johnson, Peter Carnaggio, B. Slack, Earl Davisson, Geo. Hopper, Vera McKee, Jennie Klink, Laura Jones, Manuel Pires, Pete Lunbeck, Floyd Walker, Lester Sanford, Chas. Hopkins, Harry Langlois, Mack Langlois, A. L. Bunce, R. Hart, Geo. R. Eastin, R. Corruthers, Leon Gates, Geo. Sharp and Steve Barry.

Pete Lunberg, a Santa Maria constable, claims all three were less certain about their facts the night of the disappearance, that they had, in fact, said they could not be certain of their identification or the timeline. As Kelso's trial progressed, it became clear to the jury that, although a vigilante mob in Santa Maria would gladly have lynched Kelso, there was no conclusive evidence to make him the debauched murderer that he was painted in papers. Between only pursuing one avenue of investigation and the meddling and mistakes committed, in the end, the jury's verdict was "not guilty" for William H. Kelso. A sensational crime with no sensational ending.

In the Tulare Advance-Register of July 20, 1901, young William Kelso, the accused, spoke to a reporter. This was, and would be, Kelso's story for the duration.

> **PROSECUTION CLOSED ITS CASE AT NOON**
>
> Defense Put Detective Lumbeck on the Stand to Disprove Statements Made by Prosecution's Witnesses.

Admittedly, this was his hometown paper, but there was just as much skepticism at home that Kelso was guilty as there was certainty in Santa Maria. The report went forward to call into question another local man who was part of the story: William Kincaid, a friend to Kelso since they were ten years old and acquainted with him over the twelve past years.

Kincaid, in an interview, has given his views in regard to Kelso.

It may be said that in Tulare Kincaid's reputation is about as bad as that of Kelso if, indeed, it is not owing to his associations with Kincaid that young Kelso has become wild and dissipated.

"Kelso and I had been drinking all afternoon," he said, "about 7 o'clock Kelso was very drunk. He can not drink half as much as I can without getting dead drunk, but he sobers up easily. He can lay down for an hour and get up sober. I am just the other way. It takes me a long time to get drunk, and a long time to get sober. On this night Kelso got drunk early and by the time I got drunk he was comparatively sober. I fell to sleep about 9 o'clock, I think, and do not remember anything until early next morning."

"When Kelso is drunk he is very mean and abusive and wants to fight. Yes I believe he is capable of committing the crime."

Harry Blochman was thirteen. Kelso, Kincaid, Scruggs and Pires were older, young men really, in their mid-teens to barely 20s. What kind of a row could have precipitated such a brutal crime? Someone's guilty for Harry is surely dead. Did Kelso kill him and quickly leave town? Did Kincaid kill him in a blind drunken state and throw suspicion on his childhood friend? Did two local boys fight, with one (Pires) more cunning than the other, and who then foolishly insert himself into the crime by planting evidence? Did Scruggs confuse authorities on purpose and misdirect them when he claimed he thought it was Kelso asking about the train schedule? Is there yet another element, undetected, responsible for so brutal a murder? What about Floyd Laughlin Walker, a 12-year-old classmate who suggested to Pires to plant the bloody whip stock? Was Walker the unidentified boy who claims Kelso offered him 15 cents to walk out to the bean field? Was Harry a victim of a sex crime? 120 years later, who can say?

> The difficulty encountered in getting at the truth in a trial where even a human life is at stake has been made manifest in the testimony of Manuel Pires, a 15-year-old boy of Santa Maria, in the Kelso case. Pires has just enough sense to be an ass, and, when under fire of cross-examination, proved to be a self-confessed perjurer.
>
> Before the coroner's jury and later, before the grand jury, Pires testified that he and Floyd Walker had found a blood-stained whip-stock in the bean field where the body of Harry Bolchman was was found. Both boys stated that they found it buried in the dirt a short distance from the body. A few days ago, Pires confessed that the stock had been picked up in Cook's livery stable and after having been daubed with blood at a neighboring slaughter house was taken to the bean field and buried.

Excerpt from The Independent Oct. 7, 1901

KELSO FREED BY THE JURY.

The Santa Barbara Murder Case Ends in Acquittal of Accused.

VERDICT RENDERED IN FORTY-FIVE MINUTES.

THE CHAIN OF EVIDENCE AGAINST THE COMPLAINANT LACKING IN COMPLETENESS.

What can be said for Kelso is that he was acquitted, double jeopardy would have protected him if he did want to confess after the fact and clear his conscience. In fact, such a claim was attributed to him by Harvey Ellis Scruggs. In 1906, the *Santa Maria Times* ran with a story about a deathbed confession for the murder of Harry Blochman. Supposedly, Harvey Scruggs received Kelso's deathbed confession to the crime in Tulare, Kelso's home ground. Scruggs, a local Santa Maria laborer of similar age and walk of life as Kelso, described Kelso's confession saying there was great contrition. A problem with this story is that Kelso wasn't dead. William Kelso did not die in 1906. He relocated his sister Della to Arizona, where he drank and

Manuel Pires

> "When seen later by an Independent reporter Pires was asked:
> 'What was your object in burying the whip stock in the bean field and persisting in telling a falsehood about the circumstance when you knew Kelso's life was at stake?'
> 'Oh, I don't know,' was his reply, and he would talk no further.
> There is a strong probability that Pires will be called to account by the authorities and sent to the reform school. Those who know him say he is a worthless boy, always willing to enter into an undertaking whereby someone or something will be injured. He is said to have a naturally cruel nature, delighting in torturing dumb animals. To 12-year-old Floyd Walker is attributed the conception and planning of the whipstock episode and it is probable that he, too, will be punished for perjury."

lived on until 1942, dying at the age of 64, his small community mourning him. Drunk: ten dollars or ten days seemed to be a summation of his life.

Is Scruggs just one more contributor to the Blochman case seeking attention or an unwitting accomplice? On the night of the murder, he told authorities that "a man answering the description of Kelso asked him about the train schedule." If Scruggs didn't know Kelso well enough at the time of the crime to recognize him definitively, how did he become a friend after the trial, so much so that he was in a position to receive Kelso's confession five years later? What possible motive could have compelled him to make this claim to the Blochmans?

After Kelso's acquittal no efforts were made to find other suspects. Lunbeck suggested he could produce an exposé on the murder, but, if he so intended, he never published it before his 1912 death. Whatever Lunbeck knew, it went to the grave with him when he succumbed to an injury from a horse kick to the abdomen. He is buried at Olivewood Cemetery in Riverside, CA, in an unmarked grave. Ultimately, the Blochman case left more questions than answers and was never satisfactorily solved.

Kelso death certificate 1942

Edward Walker: Killer Kid

FIENDISH MURDER BY MERE CHILD

What was supposed to have been a case of suicide at Bear Valley, San Benito county, a week ago, has turned out to be an atrocious murder, committed by a 15-year-old boy named Edward Walker, well known in this city and vicinity. Walker has been arrested and is at present in the San Benito county jail at Hollister.

Last week the lifeless body of Mrs. Ida Lang, an aged German lady, who lived alone on a little farm in Bear Valley, owned by herself, was found in a barn on the ranch. Indications pointed to suicide, and a coroner's jury decided that Mrs. Lang had taken her own life while despondent. A bullet hole through her head and a revolver with one chamber empty, lying beside the body, gave strong support to the suicide theory.

There were those, however, who were unable to believe the old lady had killed herself. Among them were Sheriff Croxon, who, after the inquest, started an investigation of his own. Sheriff Croxon suspicioned that Mrs. Lang had been murdered because the bullet hole was through the left side of her head and the revolver was found on the left side of the body. Mrs. Lang was known to be righthanded, and the sheriff could not understand how a right-handed woman could shoot herself through the left side of the head.

About this time the sheriff also learned that her house had been ransacked, that the old woman's money was missing and that young Walker had been stopping on a neighboring ranch with a family named Butterfield, had disappeared with a gun. Sheriff Croxon set out to locate Walker and sent descriptions of him to officers of the neighboring towns. He succeeded in finding Walker on a ranch near King City.

On being taken to jail Walker made a complete confession. He said that after determining to kill the old woman for her money he hid in the barn where the body was found. On the evening of Sunday, June 12, when Mrs. Lang made her appearance he stepped up behind her and shot her with the revolver. He then placed the weapon on the ground beside the body, went into the house and searched for money and valuables, and afterwards disappeared.

The young murderer was not very well rewarded as $16.25 was all the money he was able to find.

Walker is well known here and is a ward of the juvenile court. He is about 15 years old but is undersized and would readily pass for 12. He came here first from an orphan's home in Berkeley.—S. L. O. Tribune.

Santa Maria Times, July 25, 1914

Wray Case

Charleen Mildred Wray was a friendly, happy, fifteen-year-old, coed growing up in Santa Maria in 1959. The population of the town was about 20,000. There was only one high school. Most of the kids had known each other from grade school. For most of the adults in town, it was the same. Ten years previously, Santa Maria was only 10,000 people. Everyone knew everyone.

Santa Maria Police Chief Harold English said that Charleen Wray had been stabbed several times with a knife or screwdriver. The girl had been left home alone overnight on June 15th. Her sister Kathy, 17, was staying with a girlfriend, Carol Stroppini; mother Stella had been out of town on a trip to Nacimiento Lake near Paso Robles. Mrs. Wray was separated from her contractor husband, Harold L. Wray, who was living at another Santa Maria address.

It was not immediately determined if the girl had been sexually attacked. An autopsy was ordered which later confirmed no sexual assault or molestation.

Detectives reportedly checked all possible leads in the brutal, stabbing murder. Slain most probably by a screwdriver or similar object in her own home in a blitz attack as she entered the house, Charleen's death was called a mystery in the headlines.

Found early Monday by her mother, the pretty, popular, auburn-haired, high school freshman was lying in a pool of her own blood just inside the front doorway in the living room, a bag of popcorn from the movie still clutched in one hand. She had gone to a movie Sunday night with friends. That night John Simko drove the car that picked up his daughter Carol, Valerie Lanser and Charleen Wray at the Santa Maria Theatre. He took Charleen home first, arriving about 10:20-10:40 pm. He told police that he saw her enter the front door, which was seldom locked and turn on the porch lights. A light from the television flashed through the window and he drove off. He never heard anything as he left. Some neighbors reported they heard a scream.

Found lying on her back, Charleen was stabbed in the neck, in the upper abdomen, in her chest and in an upper arm. In total there were more than 20 stab wounds. There were no signs of a struggle. Robbery is ruled out as nothing in the house was touched eliminating the possibility that she interrupted a burglar. It is believed by authorities to be an acquaintance or someone well known to the victim who committed this heinous crime.

Girl Slain In Own Home

SANTA MARIA (AP) — A 15-year-old girl was found stabbed to death on the living room floor of her home today.

Police said the girl's mother, Mrs. Stella Wray, reported the apparent murder. She told them she had just returned from a trip to Paso Robles when she discovered the body in a pool of blood.

No weapon has been found, but the girl, Charlene Wray, had been stabbed several times, police said.

A 17-year-old sister, Cathy, was staying overnight with a teen-age friend, police said. The victim was believed to have been alone.

Police said they are questioning friends and neighbors, as well as Charlene's father, Harold L. Wray, who is separated from Mrs. Wray.

700 block of E. Orange Street

Mrs. Wray discovered her daughter's body shortly before 1 a.m. and drove to the police station to report the crime. The Wray telephone was out of order. Charleen was dressed in a pink sweater and black toreador pants. Her body was still warm according to a physician called to the scene. Charleen had died shortly before she was found. There were no suspects and no clues to follow according to the police. So perplexed was Chief English that he asked the county for help in solving this heinous crime. Santa Barbara County Sheriff's office sent six men to aid in the investigation. At the time there had only been three murders in Santa Maria in the previous 14 years.

A year later, there were still no leads and every likely, or unlikely, suspect has been eliminated leaving the case cold. It's hard to imagine by today's forensic standards that this crime was unsolvable. Undercover detectives mixed in Santa Maria bars, restaurants

Eight Pass 'Lie' Tests in Wray Case

Questioning Discloses No Motive

By JIM KALLENBACH
Times Staff Writer

The murderer of 15-year-old Charlene Wray was lurking in the darkened house when the girl returned from the movies Sunday night, Chief of Police Harold English theorized today.

English also said that the girl may have seen and known her assailant well, showing no fear in finding that person in the house.

Eight persons "passed" lie detector tests given recently in connection with the three-month-old Charleen Wray murder case, Chief of Police Harold English reported today.

English said the tests were given by a polygraph expert from the State Department of Justice following more than two months of undercover work by two special investigators.

The chief did not identify the eight other than to say that they were close to the case and some were adults and some were juveniles.

Miss Wray, 15, was murdered in her home the evening of June 14 after returning from the movies. She was viciously stabbed by an assailant who police theorize was lurking in the darkened house at 720 E. Orange St. when the victim entered.

English said two homicide experts, Charles Ryken, of the Alameda County district attorney's office, and William Cummings, of Los Angeles, have been working undercover on the case for more than two months.

He said the two were arranged for on his request by District Attorney Vern Thomas and Deputy District Attorney Thomas P. Weldon, of Santa Barbara County. The two circulated throughout the city during the past months, visiting bars, restaurants and all likely sources that might develop a solid lead on the case, English said.

Despite the apparent failure to develop anything new in the case, work on it is continuing. English said one of the investigators will return to do more work on the case and he and his department are constantly working on the case.

The lie detector tests were given by J. F. McVarish, of Sacramento.

English also reported that the weapon used in the slaying has never been discovered.

and hotels listening to local chatter, hoping for a lead. Nothing developed in over six months of surveillance. In 2000 a murdered 46-year-old man and former classmate of Wray was tagged as her murderer after someone looking for a reduction in his own prison sentence supposedly heard a confession in 1990 from Rick Perea. He would have been 15 years old at the time of the murder,

Proposed confessor of the crime, Rick Perea, his 1959 photo from SMH yearbook.

the same as Charleen and in the same graduation year. He was a student athlete, actively involved in school and, most importantly, without an obvious motive. Why this man, also a murder victim, would be presented to the Wray family as resolving her case was a travesty unless there was more that hasn't been revealed.

Most of the evidence points to a misidentification murder. Charleen was not the target. She is so similar in stature to her mother that the original theory is that the father mistakenly killed Charleen, not his estranged wife. All focus was on this theory.

Harold L. Wray doesn't make a good suspect by today's standards. He was at the same movie as his daughter albeit not seated with her. He would be moving on the same timeline as she was. Getting from the movie theatre to the Orange Street house, premeditatedly planning to kill your estranged spouse and knowing your daughter also left the movie at the same time, isn't good planning. Also, choosing (with premeditation) a screwdriver as the best murder tool seems a stretch too. Men favor hammers, guns and bats. Remember, he's planning to kill her in this scenario. He comes in stealthily with his weapon of choice and stands in the dark on the other side of the door. Who would choose a screwdriver for a premeditated murder? No weapon was ever recovered.

So, what we know is that it was first believed that Stella Wray was the likely target. The means of murder would make it a crime of passion, but there is no sexual element. The question next to ask would be "is there a woman with a motive for attacking Stella A. Wray?" Knives, ice picks and poisons area women's tools of murder.

All we can conclude is that whoever committed this murder got clean away.

Harold English, Police Chief

Eileen Effie Baker Case

A brutal attack in a Santa Maria home with no visible motive caused tensions to rise as residents remembered the Wray murder case of 1959. Eileen Baker lay near death January 2, 1968, after being brutally beaten and choked in her home at 1309 N. Lincoln Street. She was found by her husband lying unconscious on her stomach on the master bedroom floor around 5:20 p.m. Police reported there were no signs of a struggle and no forced entry in to the home.

Mrs. Baker, 40, an attractive honey blonde was listed in very-critical condition at Marian Hospital following six-hour brain surgery. At the time of the attack, she was wearing street clothes and was not sexually assaulted.

Eileen Baker was hit several times at the top and back of her head with a large claw hammer and choked with a piece of drapery cord. The hammer, covered with blood and hair, was located in the house underneath a sectional couch in the couples living room. A one-foot length of drapery cord was tied in a knot around her neck. The cord was not from draperies in the house. The hammer did belong to the Bakers and was normally kept in the garage. Police Captain Lloyd Britell, chief of detectives, said the case was puzzling because there was no sign of a struggle, nothing in the home was disturbed, nothing stolen. The entire incident occurred inside the bedroom, and there was no forcible entry. The time of the beating was placed between 4 and 5 p.m. The hammer and cord were sent to a Sacramento crime lab for analysis.

The timeline of the attack was established by neighborhood testimony. Baker arrived home about 4 p.m. and was greeted by her young next-door neighbor, six-year-old Derek Biro. He stopped to say "hello" as she pulled her car up to the garage. It was *Times* delivery boy, Ronald Pardo, who spotted the drapes move back as he turned to check his aim toward the porch at approximately 4:50 p.m. He was uncertain if he saw a man or woman, only movement.

The force of the attack has caused the detective to rule out an attack by a woman although it was accepted that a woman of considerable strength and coordination could have accomplished the blows. The assailant remains unknown and, so far, there have been no other clues beyond the cord which originated outside of the home. Baker remained in a comma providing no witness to her attacker for the next 37 days.

Police Capt. Lloyd Britell, Det. Joe Centeno and Chief Harold English Reveal Arrest of Beating Suspect

February 22, 1968, Fred L. Shelby, Jr., a 6-foot 2-inch, seventeen-year-old Santa Maria High School senior was arrested for the assault and attempted murder in the hammer and strangulation attack on Eileen Baker. Shelby was taken into custody at 2 p.m. on school grounds and booked at 4:35 p.m. on the twin charges. Police assured the community that Shelby was the lone assailant but gave no details as to his motive at the time of his arrest. It was reported that the motive would remain "secret." Gossip shared suggested that young Shelby was enraged over an alleged affair between Baker and Shelby, Sr. This motive could not be confirmed. Shelby lived about a block away, at 209 Sunset, and was considered a "good kid" without prior brushes with the law. Shelby, Jr., is the son of Freddie Lee and Helen Shelby, owners of Freddie's TV service.

Freddie L. Shelby, Jr., confessed to authorities and was charged in juvenile court. He was sentenced to the California Youth Authority until his 25th birthday and then faced an indefinite period of parole.

Fred L. Shelby Jr. yearbook picture, Santa Maria High School.

Fortunately for Shelby, Eileen Baker beat the odds and made a miraculous recovery. Her mental faculties were not compromised and within eight months she could walk with support and climb a few stairs. She was partially paralyzed on her right side, but each day brought a little more mobility.

After the gripping headlines subsided, both victim and assailant had survived this horrific crime, but no one's life was ever fully restored.

On April 24, 2000, Eileen Baker, age 72, passed away at her home in Suey Creek Road, Santa Maria, after a brief illness. She was born in 1927 in Montana and moved with her family to Boulder City, Nevada, where she completed her high school education. During World War II she worked at Norton Air Force Base in San Bernardino. She moved to Sacramento in the late 1940s and attended junior college majoring in art. She loved to paint in water colors and oils. She met her husband of 43 years, Robert M. Baker, while she worked as a fashion model and instructor for Coronet of California. They came to Santa Maria for her husband Bob to take a Santa Barbara County Fair job. In 1960 she opened a mosaic tile shop, which she operated until 1964. She continued her art education at Allan Hancock College until the time of her attack. A long convalescent period followed.

Fundraisers were held all over town to help with hospital expenses for Eileen Baker.

Trouble found Freddie Lee Shelby, Jr., again, at age 28 when he was arrested and charged with sex counts and assault. Police arrested him at his 200 block West Sunset Street address on a warrant charging him with suspicion of assault with a deadly weapon, forcible rape, and three other counts in connection with an attack on a Santa Maria woman on May 10, 1979.

Shelby was arrested at his place of work, a television repair shop in the 200 block of North Broadway. According to Detective Bill Ryle, Shelby met the 23-year-old victim in a North Broadway bar, Rick's Rancho, on the evening of May 9. She charged that he invited her to see a television set he wanted to trade. The victim was struck in the back of the head with a pair of vice grips in the bar parking lot and forced into Shelby's van. She claims that she was taken to the repair shop where he forcibly raped and sexually assaulted her in several ways.

Shelby was found not guilty in a Santa Barbara court. The venue had been moved because the defendant had been prosecuted before in this jurisdiction. A claim for $1,573,000 was filed against the Santa Maria City police department, the city and county. The circumstances giving rise to this claim were: Freddie Lee Shelby, Jr., was convicted in 1968 of beating Eileen Baker. He served his full sentence as imposed by the court. Shelby was then wrongfully prosecuted for raping a Santa Maria prostitute who had agreed to sexual favors. He was acquitted. "That whole prosecution was entirely motivated by the malice of the Santa Maria police department who felt Shelby was not punished severely enough for his prior crime 10 years ago," suggested his attorney.

S. M. TIMES - 04-09-1980

Shelby found not guilty of assault-rape

Freddie Lee Shelby Jr. of Santa Maria was found not-guilty of charges of assault and forceable rape in a trial that ended Tuesday in Santa Barbara.

The trial was moved from Santa Maria in a change of venue.

Shelby was arrested by city police detectives last May 16, on a warrant charging him with the crimes in connection with the attack upon a 23-year-old woman on May 10. At that time detectives said he met the woman in a North Broadway bar.

Judge Arden Jensen presided in the two-week superior court trial and Phil Kohn of the district attorney's office prosecuted the case.

Dystiny McKenna Myers

First degree murder, is the charge that will face those who brutally murdered fifteen-year-old Dystiny Myers of Santa Maria. Found September 26, 2010, she was burned beyond recognition and buried in a hand dug pit. Her charred body was discovered by firefighters who responded to a brush fire in the 5300 block of Parkhill Road off Highway 58 in northern San Luis Obispo County. Five people were charged with this horrific crime.

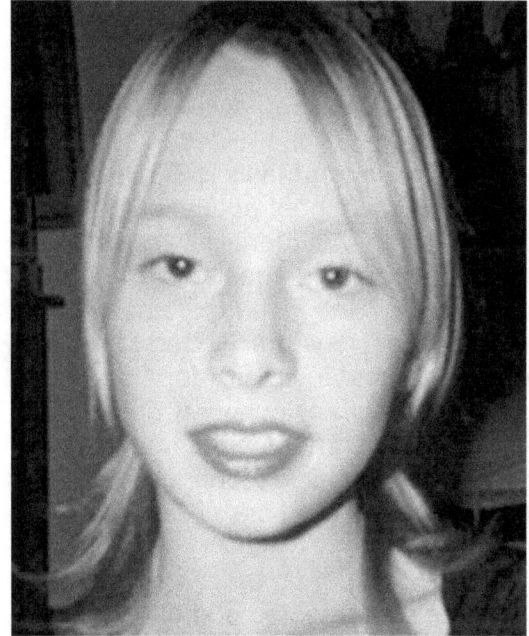

Dystiny was born in Tucson, Arizona, on August 18, 1995. She had lived in Santa Maria since she was five months old. Dystiny attended Adams Elementary; Alvin Elementary; Robert Bruce, where she graduated 6th grade; and finally El Camino Junior High, where she completed the 8th grade. Dystiny was being raised by her grandmother, Kathlene Rose Clark.

Two of the murderers were a mother-son combo from Nipomo. The mother, Rhonda Maye Wisto, said the girl disrespected her and wanted her gone. She feared Dystiny knew too much about the methamphetamine house that Wisto, her son, and several other associates were running, to just let her leave. According to Wisto's cell mate, Tabatha Brown, who testified against Wisto, the older woman felt there was no way she'd face justice because runaways like Dystiny go missing all the time, that bad things happen, no one would miss her. She confided many grotesque details to Brown. Forensic investigators found a glove shoved down Myers' throat, sweatpants tied around her neck and skull fractures. One of her eyes was gouged out of its socket, and there was severe bruising throughout her body. It was also revealed that York and Dystiny shared a bed. His mother didn't want him accused of statutory rape at a later date.

Wisto, who believed she would never see the inside of a courtroom, was sentenced to life without the possibility of parole.

Jeanine West, SLO County Sheriff's forensic specialist shows bat to jury, on which York's fingerprints were recovered. The bat also tested positive for blood.

The death penalty was laid on the table for Ty Michael Hill, 28, of Santa Maria, for planning the brutal homicide. The gruesome details of mechanical asphyxiation and blunt force trauma were catalyst enough to seek capital punishment, but Dystiny was also drugged, beaten, duct taped, hog-tied and stuffed in a duffle bag, before her lifeless body was set ablaze along Highway 101.

To avoid the death penalty, Hill pleaded guilty to first degree murder and accepted the sentence of life without the possibility of parole. Hill had committed all of the acts of which only one was required to qualify for a capital charge in his First Degree Murder indictment.

Hill

First-Degree Murder

According to Penal Code 189 PC, a prosecutor can charge first-degree murder when someone kills another human being by:

1. using a destructive device or explosive, a weapon of mass destruction, or poison
2. inflicting torture
3. a willful, deliberate, and premeditated killing
4. committing felony-murder

or

5. lying in wait.

At trial, Jason Adam Greenwell, told the storyline and provided a timeline for the night of the homicide. Dystiny, a runaway, had decided to leave the Wisto's house and return to Santa Maria. The teen had gathered her few belongings from the house and came out to the garage to tell the group good-bye. Greenwell said that everyone paused at that point, and Ty Hill instructed the men to go into the house and put on dark clothing and rubber gloves.

Wisto and Hill had premeditatedly decided that Dystiny knew too much about the illegal activities conducted at the Mars Court house. It was a haven for methamphetamine users as well as a local hub where other narcotics could be bought and sold. It was alleged that Wisto's had connections to a White Supremacist group as well as ties to a local Mexican gang. Letting the girl walk out wasn't an option. The crew beat her with a baseball bat and stomped her. The teen cried out, according to Greenwell to, "tell my mother I love her." Greenwell testified that Hill and Wisto had discussed how to get rid of a body days prior to the savage murder. Hill made a list, and Wisto gathered the goods is how Greenwell described it.

Greenwell demonstrated for the jury how Hill bound a drugged Dystiny Myers before she was beaten. He also testified he saw Hill set Dystiny on fire. He was unsure if she was already dead.

In California law, second-degree murder is defined as the unlawful killing of a human being that is done without deliberation and premeditation but with malice aforethought. Greenwell, 21, as part of a plea bargain, agreed to testify truthfully about the events of that night and to plead guilty to a second-degree murder charge. He was sentenced to fifteen years to life with the possibility of parole.

Greenwell's Current Parole Status

The fifth defendant in the case was Cody Lane Miller, 20 of Fresno. After the killing, while at the burn site, Miller was beaten with shovels by York, Hill and Greenwell in an attempt to kill him when the group suspected him of being a police informant. Miller escaped into the brush and remained hidden until firefighters, responding to a 911 roadside fire call, spotted him running towards them out of the dark claiming this was a murder scene. He led investigators to the body and confessed the details of the homicide. Miller admitted to pushing the glove into the runaway's mouth and

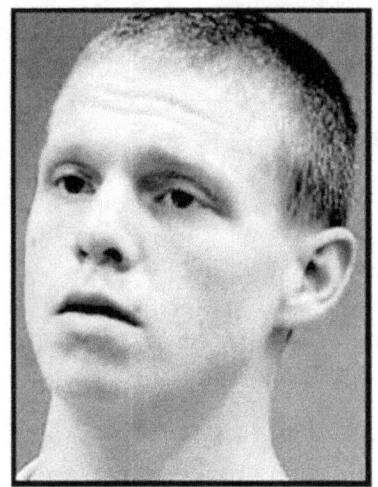

punching her several times. He claimed he was coerced into it by the other defendants. He also reported being raped by Ty Michael Hill with a baseball bat the day of the murder. At the time of the original arraignment Miller was in hospital being treated for various injuries.

Miller initially agreed to testify for a plea arrangement that would be 39 years, 4 months, and the possibility of parole. Later, he decided that he didn't deserve the deal and was sentenced immediately to life in prison without parole. He told his attorney he didn't believe he deserved forgiveness for his part in the murder. In June, 2016, Cody Lane Miller committed suicide in his prison cell. The correctional institution in Tehachapi, where he was serving his life sentence, found him dead. Miller did not have a cell mate, and his cause of death was ruled suicide by asphyxiation.

Dystiny Myers was full of energy, and she enjoyed singing and performing at every chance she got: at home, in public and in church. She was often singing the lead in many productions in the children's choir at Pacific Christian Church and enjoyed snow camp trips with her youth group. Dystiny was full of life, and the love she carried in her heart was known by all those who knew her well according to family and friends. Dystiny was a child full of life and promise, but she took a bigger bite of life than she could swallow.

Inmate Name	GREENWELL, JASON ADAM
CDCR Number	AP5598
Parole Eligible Date (Month/Year)	09/2021

Pending Board Actions

Date	Action	Status
November 18, 2021	Parole Suitability Hearing	Tentative date for parole suitability hearing

Past Board Actions

Date	Action	Outcome
December 26, 2018	Consultation	Inmate's consultation was conducted

Statistically Speaking

Accidents and homicide are the leading causes of death for those 15–24 years of age, each accounting for 34.2% and 32.9%, respectively, of all deaths. The third leading cause of death in this age group is suicide.

City of Santa Maria

In 2018, the City of Santa Maria experienced an almost 16 percent decrease in overall Part I Crimes, which are categorized as Violent Crimes and Property Crimes. There are four crimes in each category that all police agencies are required to report.

Within the Violent Crime category, homicides doubled from three in 2017 to six in 2018. The homicide number is on average with our five-year average as well as the national average for a city of our size.

Forcible rape numbers increased by less than 1 percent from 62 to 63. Aggravated assaults also increased by almost 5 percent from 266 to 279. However, robbery decreased from 164 to 161. Overall, violent crime for 2018 increased by almost three percent from 2017.

With respect to Property Crime, burglaries are down 22 percent from 481 to 393 and larceny/theft decreased 22 percent from 1,330 to 1,033. Motor vehicle thefts also saw a decrease of 17 percent from 702 to 580. Arson numbers did see an increase from 12 to 24. Overall, Property Crime is down almost 20 percent.

Numbers mean very little if you are the victim of a crime. Numbers are a way to measure if society is acting in an effective manner to protect citizens as a whole.

This data reflects the 2020 calendar year and was released from the FBI in September, 2021

Statistic	Reported incidents	Santa Maria /100k people	California /100k people	National /100k people
Total crime	3,306	3,057	2,581	2,346
Murder	2	1.8	5.6	6.5
Rape	81	74.9	34.2	38.4
Robbery	179	165.5	113.6	73.9
Assault	572	528.9	288.7	279.7
Violent crime	834	771	442	388
Burglary	328	303.3	369.7	314.2
Theft	1,114	1,030.2	1,341.7	1,398.0
Vehicle theft	1,030	952.5	427.6	246.0
Property crime	2,472	2,286	2,139	1,958

Chapter 3: Domestic Violence

Those hearty pilgrims who voyaged to the New World brought a boatload of innovative ideas with them. It was a motivating factor, a new world, a new way of life. In 1641 a legal code, *Body of Liberties of the Massachusetts Bay,* was established by Puritan colonists in New England declaring that a married woman should be "free from bodily correction or stripes by her husband." New Hampshire and Rhode Island also explicitly banned wife-beating in their criminal codes.

> ### Murder and Suicide.
>
> Last Sunday night word was brought to town that two dead bodies were in the road a few feet from the upper Suey gate on the Cuyama road.
>
> Justice Morris, acting coroner, empaneled a jury and left town at 2 o'clock Monday morning to look into the cause and bring the dead home. The investigation proved that the couple were man and wife, and both were cold in death, with no eyewitness to the deed.
>
> The man, J. M. Hamilton, was at work for the Sugar Company, but has only been here about ten days. He and his wife were boarding at the Crosby house. Sunday morning they left town to visit a daughter of Mrs. Hamilton, by her first husband, Mrs. Juan Olivera, living on the Dutard ranch, about 20 miles east of here. They finished their visit and started to return about 3 p.m. When they left, Juan Olivera and wife strolled out to view their crops and within an hour or thereabouts their attention was attracted by rumbling wheels and in a few seconds they recognized the horse and buggy recently driven from their door. Catching the horse, they turned him round and drove rapidly down the road, soon coming in sight of the scene of the tragedy. When they arrived Hamilton was yet standing, he having used the knife on himself only after they came in sight. Mrs. Olivera asked him a question but received no answer and in a few seconds he fell. Finding the life fled from the mother, here body already cold and stiffening, they sought help. In their absence Hamilton arose and fell again a few feet from where he first lay and there is where the coroner's jury found them both.
>
> A verdict of murder and suicide was quickly reached and arrangements made to bring both bodies to town for burial.
>
> Hamilton was a member of our Whittier lodge of Odd Fellows and the home lodge took charge of the remains and buried him and his wife in one grave.
>
> The trouble that caused the tragedy, if any existed, was of long standing for there were never happily married and the wife's life had been repeatedly threatened. It would seem that the last act was premeditated as Hamilton sharpened a paper-hanger's knife Saturday after he quit work and took it with him on the visit, but for a full hour, or longer, after cutting the throat of his wife he delayed the completion of the crime, and wrote a note stating "I done this," with a lot of instructions which his own blood almost washed out.

However, there were also legal systems that implicitly accepted wife-beating as a husband's right. Many states transferred jurisdiction in divorce cases from their legislatures to their judicial system, and the legal recourse available to battered women increasingly became divorce on grounds of cruelty and suing for assault. This placed a great burden of proof on the woman, as she needed to demonstrate to a court that her life was at risk. In 1824 a court ruling in Mississippi established a positive right to wife-beating in *State v. Bradley*, a precedent which would hold sway in common law for decades to come. It provided that a man was entitled to enforce "domestic discipline" by striking his wife with a whip or stick no wider than the judge's thumb. In a later case in North Carolina (*State v. Rhodes*, 1868), the defendant was found to have struck his wife "with a switch about the size of his fingers"; the judge found the man not guilty due to the switch being smaller than a thumb.

By the late 19th century, most American states had outlawed wife-beating; some had severe penalties such as forty lashes or imprisonment for offenders. The first known use of the term domestic violence, meaning violence in the home, was in an address to the Parliament of the United Kingdom by Jack Ashley in 1973.

Domestic violence is violence or other abuse in a familial setting, such as you might find in a marriage or cohabitation. Domestic violence is intimate partner abuse, which is committed by one of the people in a relationship against the other person and can take place in heterosexual or same-sex relationships or between former spouses or partners. In its broadest sense, domestic violence also involves violence against children, teenagers, parents, or the elderly. It can take multiple forms, including physical, verbal, emotional, economical or sexual abuse, which can range from subtle, coercive forms to marital rape or violent physical abuse such as choking, beating, disfigurement or death.

Haslam-Low Case

Young Haslam

Santa Maria, May 27, 1956, Arthur W. Haslam, a 64-year-old, prominent merchant, was late for work. His brother and business partner, Fred, went to seek him out at his East Camino Colegio home at about 10:00 a.m. on Sunday morning.

It was a blood-spattered scene that awaited on the other side of the door. There had been a scuffle with bloody shoe tracks and bloodstains in the hallway and the bathroom. Art Haslam had been slain in what could only be called "a rage." City police arriving on scene, after the brother's notification, find his body on its side, on the floor, knifed to death.

Find 2 Calif. Men Stabbed to Death

SANTA MARIA (U.P) — The bodies of Arthur Haslam, 65, and David Story Low, 28, were found in their home here Monday in what sheriff's deputies believed to be a murder and suicide.

The coroner's office said Haslam was found with stab wounds in the chest and Low was found a short distance away with both wrists cut and his throat slashed. A 10-inch carving knife was found next to Low's body.

In the bathroom, his head hanging over the sink was David Story Low, 37. Six-foot two-inches tall, Low's body was seated in a chair with his head hanging over the bathroom sink. He had apparently slit his own throat and both of his wrists. Investigators would need to determine who killed whom.

The murder weapon was found on the floor near Low's body, a 13½ inch carving knife with a nine-inch curved blade. Wounds to the chest caused Haslam's death sometime between Saturday midnight and 3.a.m. Sunday morning.

Santa Barbara pathologist Dr. John T. Blanchard examined the bodies and determined cause of death. Both men bled to death. Blanchard further determined that Haslam was the murder victim, Low a suicide. This case of murder-suicide appears motivated by a domestic dispute.

Haslam was born August 11, 1891, in Santa Maria. He was a lifelong resident. He was a member of the Knights of Pythias No. 90, the Santa Maria Club, Marshall M. Braden American Legion Post No. 56 (charter member). He was a past commander of the local American Legion Post and a World War I veteran. Haslam attended local schools and was one of the owners of W. A. Haslam & Company, incorporated, a local dry goods store that was a mainstay in the community for several generations.

Low, born in Boston, Massachusetts, grew up in the New England area and served in World War II. His father, Fletcher Low, came to Santa Maria and took his son home to Hanover, New Hampshire where he was buried in Dartmouth College Cemetery.

Epps Case

A double death occurred June 1965 when a family argument climaxed with a murder-suicide. Herschel A. Epps, 44, borrowed a .22 caliber pump-action rifle from a family member and invaded the home of his estranged wife. Epps was intoxicated and had been barred from the family home and his children when he was drinking. He shot Lena Faye Epps in the heart killing her instantly and then turned the weapon on himself, discharging it into his head behind his right ear. Three of four children were in the house at the time. They escaped through a bedroom window to a neighbor's screaming, "Daddy has shot Momma!"

S.M. Man Slays Wife, Kills Self

The family home was at 410 N. DeJoy, and both bodies were in the living room. Epps was a plumber and a heavy drinker. There had been numerous altercations at the home. Mrs. Epps never pursued charges, but she was seeking a divorce. Epps had told other family that he couldn't stand the thought of it. Mrs. Epps had been granted an interlocutory decree of divorce in April.

Both are buried in the Santa Maria Cemetery.

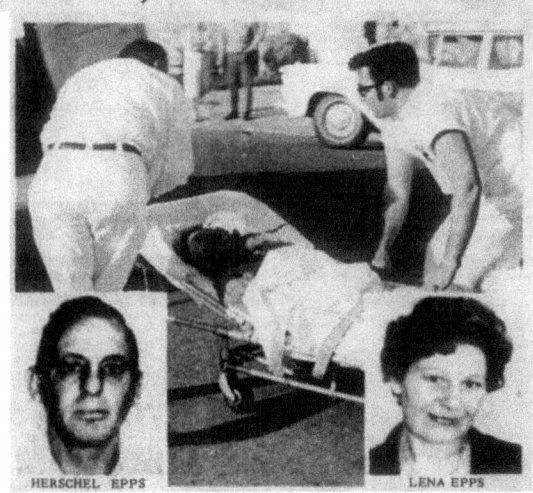

Schlager Case

Schlager pleads innocent to kidnap, murder of wife

The headline in April of 1977 was a big one. The accused were young. Eric Francis Schlager, 22, pled not guilty to the charges, but his 22-year-old wife, Kathy June Schlager, was dead by a gunshot to the back of the head. They were divorced but a bitter custody battle had darkened the process. There was an accused accomplice, 20-year-old Mathew James Stevens.

The two were suspected of kidnapping Mrs. Schlager, who was the mother of two young girls, from her 1044-C West Cook Street apartment and driving her to a location on the Nipomo Mesa where she was killed. Her body was recovered on November 17, 1976, after Stevens allegedly confessed and told law enforcement where to find the body.

First reported missing by family and friends, the young devoted mother was not expected to be found alive and she wasn't. She was found dead in a eucalyptus grove five days after her disappearance. The prosecution painted a devastating picture of the events. The defense claimed deals have been made, and that the truth of the evening in question is obscured. The case is presented to a jury of six men and six women. The murder was premeditated and that, in fact, Schlager had tried to hire others to murder his ex-wife for $500.

"Kathy was afraid of him, but she told me just last Friday that she still loved him." Davis revealed.

Barbara Davis was a close friend of Kathy Schlager and knew her well.

The night began with games of pool and cocaine. Schlager first attacked Kathy at her apartment, overwhelmed her and knocked her unconscious. Stevens claimed he saw blood coming from her mouth and her eyes staring blankly into space. Stevens then kicked her violently in the throat and legs before picking her up and dumping her into the trunk of his car. Schlager was winded from the fight.

They headed up Highway 1 to the Nipomo Mesa where the Schlagers use to live in a trailer but pulled onto a deserted dirt road. They opened the trunk and Kathy, to their joint surprise, stepped out of the confines of the trunk under her own power, although quite dazed and disoriented.

Schlager proceeded to lead her into the dark away from the car. Stevens informed her that "Eric is taking you to meet God." Eric shot, missed and returned to Steven's location to get an additional bullet. He said that he would put the next one in her brain. His weapon is a .22 caliber sawed off rifle.

Eric Schlager in handcuffs.

The deed done, the two men drove to a cliff overlooking the ocean at Shell Beach, and the gun and some bloody clothing are flung into the water. The body was found five days later when Stevens confessed to San Luis authorities. Schlager and Stevens were both jailed. Both did a lot of talking which was soon regretted.

Schlager sentenced to life

Eric Francis Schlager was sentenced to life in state prison by Judge Royce Lewellen this morning for the execution - style murder of his estranged wife.

Trying to blame drug use and loss of memory, Schlager withdrew his confession forcing the authorities to make a deal with Stevens, who agreed and received leniency for his testimony. Much mockery was made of the night the suspects were questioned despite the fact both confessed, and the gun had even been recovered on the beach. The jury would determine the murder was willful, deliberate and premeditated. Eric Schlager was sentenced to life in prison. Judge S. Jon Gudmunds named Kathy Schlager's sister and brother-in-law

Phyllis and Allison Kelly as guardians for the two children, Tina Rene and Crystal.

Schlager's time is scheduled to be served in Chino State Prison. He received credit for 176 days served in county jail. He is eligible for parole in 6.5 years. He remarried in a jailhouse ceremony to Catherine A. Winslow, 16 years old. They divorced in December 1980.

May 1992, Schlager was denied parole and had to wait in the California Men's Colony for another chance in two years.

SM murderer denied parole

May 1999, Schlager was in Folsom Prison having completed 22 years on his life sentence. October 9, 2007, Eric Francis Schlager has died.

Matthew James Stevens, the 21-year-old Atascadero man who was Schlager's accomplice in the murder of Kathy June Schlager was sentenced to state prison for a term of about two years.

Mathew James Stevens the admitted accomplice.

Hunt-Throckmorton Case

James Craig Hunt called the murder, "a terrible mistake. I am not an evil person, just a man that got very scared and did not use better judgement."

The courts hear such statements regularly. In imposing a sentence, it must be unimaginable to the family of slain members to hear such things pronounced. I'm sorry doesn't bring the dead back or restore families to each other. This case is so frustrating because it characterizes a very typical representation of domestic violence. A partner does something horrible and apologizes for it, over and over and over. When the abused party tries to break the cycle, it can often end with death. It took a month for police to gather the evidence needed to arrest James Craig Hunt for murder. It was circumstantial, at best. Anne Throckmorton had vanished into thin air on July 18, 1993. The worst of it is that Hunt should have been arrested for drunk driving, DUI, the evening of her

Search continues for missing woman

Authorities continue to search for a Santa Maria woman who mysteriously disappeared one week ago.

Anne Throckmorton, 26, vanished from her residence in the 1000 block of North School Street, leaving her four-year-old child behind.

Throckmorton, who worked at the Santa Maria YMCA, is 5-foot-5, 120 pounds, with sandy brown hair and eyes.

Anyone with information is asked to call police at 928-3781.

■ MISSING PERSONS CASE

San Luis Obispo Sheriff's dive team members load air tanks into boats at Twitchell Reservoir.

Searchers find body
Woman recovered from creek may be Anne Throckmorton

murder. The police released him and a few hours later, he murdered his estranged domestic partner, Anne M. Throckmorton, 26. She had been a resident in Santa Maria for more than 25 years. Anne had attended local schools including Fesler Junior High where she was captain of the drill team. She started high school at Santa Maria but was a graduate of Delta High School. She worked for four years as associate photographer at J.C. Penney Company in the portrait studio. She had recently been promoted to office manager at the Santa Maria YMCA.

James Craig Hunt was not a positive influence. He had been lurking around Anne for more than ten years. That night in October when he was stopped by police, he was on felony probation, had crank and an open bottle of tequila in his truck, and was driving under the influence, but somehow, he walked away from authorities that night. He took the mercy he had received and turned it to rage against someone he maintained he loved. Hunt and Throckmorton had dated on and off for over ten years. They had a child together, Chelsey Lynn Hunt. Hunt blamed Throckmorton's death on her taunting him over another man. He claimed he strangled her in the heat of passion as she teased him about sleeping with someone else.

An argument ensued at Throckmorton's 1015 N. School Street home. Hunt claimed he blacked out. He awakened to find her lifeless body in his arms, his hands around her throat. He had strangled her to death.

After the murder, Hunt moved her corpse to a remote area at the Pismo Dunes, poured diesel fuel on it, and set her on fire. Several days later, finding that charred portions remained, Hunt retrieved the unburned pieces, wrapped them in garbage bags and drove to a bridge where he threw them into Twitchell Reservoir. Through the trial, the more the family heard the details of Throckmorton's last moments and how her body was treated, the pain and suffering multiplied. Her aunt, Linda Compton, admitted, "increase knowledge (about the crime) increases our pain."

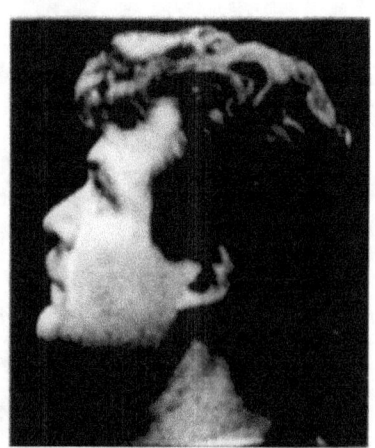

James Craig Hunt, 31

Because Hunt hid the body, the family lived the tragedy of a "missing person." A missing person is a person who has disappeared and whose status as alive or dead cannot be determined. They waited for word.

For weeks, authorities trudged through hills, dried creek beds and rocky, dusty trails in remote areas around Garey, Santa Ynez, Guadalupe, along Highway 166 and 101 and parts in-between.

The Sheriff's department finally recovered what they believed were the remains of Anne Throckmorton. She was eventually identified by her dental records.

Hunt had tried for a plea bargain during this extended period that she was missing. Ultimately a lesser plea was not accepted by the judge. Showing little emotion in the courtroom, Hunt blamed Throckmorton's death on a bad temper and his addiction to alcohol and drugs. Prosecutor Christie Schultz called Hunt a cold-blooded killer. Part of his attempt at a plea bargain included him disclosing the location of Throckmorton's body. Hunt resisted this and, in fact, did not himself disclose what he had done with her body. He shared information with a cell mate, Joseph Edwards, who informed the authorities to where they might search to find remains. Hunt hoped the body was gone, unrecognizable, unidentifiable.

In missing person's cases where foul play is known, pleas in exchange for the body are often made. Closure for the family is of paramount importance and, in many cases, the murderer will continue to claim the person is alive and just hiding out to make him look guilty. A charge of murder is also much easier to prosecute with a body available to tell its grisly story: forensic evidence is available; the cause of death and a timeline may be established. Hunt wanted to obscure as much as possible. He tried pleading guilty to involuntary manslaughter. He would have served less than eleven years but he never led authorities to Anne Throckmorton's remains and made an allocution statement to his crime in open court. He continued to force the family to suffer with her disappearance and authorities to spend resources trying to locate her.

Anne Throckmorton and James C. Hunt pose in December, 1988, with newborn daughter Chelsea.

Throckmorton's family and friends wanted the death sentence. Hunt had committed murder because Anne Throckmorton wanted him out of her life, he had brutalized her and covered it up; in every way he had tried to avoid the consequences of his crime. The family believed that Hunt's actions spoke his motive clearly, "If I can't have her, no one else will."

Hunt was sentenced to 15-years-to-life in state prison for the second-degree murder of his estranged girlfriend, burning her body, and throwing her remains off the J.J. Hollister bridge. He received an additional 5 years for the probation violation involving cocaine sales. Second-degree murder is defined as murder that is not premeditated or murder that is caused by the offender's reckless conduct that displays an obvious lack of concern for human life.

This is James Craig Hunt's current status: although sentenced to 20 years, he has been denied parole five times; if he were to be released in 2026, he will have been in prison for 33 years.

San Quentin is a California Department of Corrections and Rehabilitation state prison for men located north of San Francisco in the unincorporated place of San Quentin in Marin County.

The first inmates arrived in July 1852. San Quentin is the oldest prison in California. The state's only death row for male inmates, the largest in the United States, is located at San Quentin. It has a gas chamber, but since 1996, executions at the prison have been carried out by lethal injection; the prison has not performed an execution since 2006.

San Quentin is referred to as "The Arena" by prisoners.

Brian Keith Reid

Labor Day weekend 2012 in Orcutt Community Park, a family barbeque goes terribly wrong. Brian Reid shot and killed his father William Forrest Reid, 73, and seriously wounded his mother, Pamela, 66. The couple were Orcutt residents. Supposedly gathering for a late celebration of Brian's 40th birthday, the situation turned deadly when he produced a .40 caliber Glock and shot both his parents.

What precipitated the tragedy is possibly more disturbing. Brian Reid had been deliberating on an impending charge against his father for molesting Brian's three daughters. The allegations began back in 2005. Brittany Reid, 20, reported that her grandfather, known as Forrest Reid had molested her and her two sisters for years. Breanna Reid, 24, claimed her father's personality changed after learning that his daughters had been sexually abused by his father Forrest Reid. "He became angry and distant," she said.

It seemed that the weight of this absorbed him and took a toll on his marriage as well. Brian and Patricia Reid reportedly argued about it at their home in Arizona. The

2012 arraignment, photo by Daniel Dreifuss/*Santa Maria Times* Staff

situation was creating tension and stress with other family members. According to Brian's daughters, Pamela Reid wanted to keep it quiet, unknown to Brian's other siblings. There was a suggestion by Brian's wife, Patricia, that he began abusing prescription and synthetic drugs.

Pamela Reid, at trial 2015

Pamela Reid had, in her son Brian's estimation, been trying to get her granddaughters to not pursue charges and to be silent about the abuse. She sent bible verses and instructions on the value of forgiveness. Brian seemingly felt his mother was on the wrong side of the issue.

Just five days before the shooting Forrest Reid admitted to authorities in Arizona, where Brian's family lived, that he had inappropriately touched at least one of his granddaughters. No charges had been filed at the time.

Forrest Reid died at the Orcutt Community Park on September 3, 2012. Pamela Reid received five wounds but survived telling authorities at the scene that her son was the shooter. Brian Reid fled in his black jeep after the shooting eventually going to the Marian Medical Center himself for an undisclosed reason He was arrested without incident at the hospital on charges of murder and attempted murder.

> Commander Kendall Greene of the Santa Maria Police department took a statement from Pamela Reid on scene believing she might not survive.

> Pamela Reid told Greene that her son had perpetrated the attack. When he asked if she knew why, Greene said she nodded and said that her husband was going to testify, and alluded that Brian Reid had molested one or more of his daughters.

Brian Reid and his mother told differing accounts of what transpired that Monday, Labor Day. She suggested that Brian was blackmailing them. Brian said that his parents had threatened to turn the table and set him up as the molester. Both refuted the other's statements. However, Commander Greene did say Pamela Reid changed her statement.

The allegations first came to light in October 2005, after Breanna Reid told a friend that her grandfather had touched her while he thought she was sleeping when her grandparents visited the family in Arizona.

Her parents subsequently found out that William Reid had molested their middle daughter, Brittney Reid, on multiple occasions while she visited him and Pamela Reid at their Orcutt home and while they vacationed at Sequoia National Park and in San Francisco.

The timing and level of rage was argued. However, some light was shed when it was suggested that younger granddaughters might become at risk. Ultimately Brian Reid agreed to a plea deal to avoid the possibility of life in prison. He was found guilty of voluntary manslaughter and attempted murder without premeditation. Brian Reid had already been in custody for two years and eight months when the sentence of 24 years and 4 months was pronounced. He will have to serve 85% before he will be eligible for parole.

Forrest Reid was never charged with any crime.

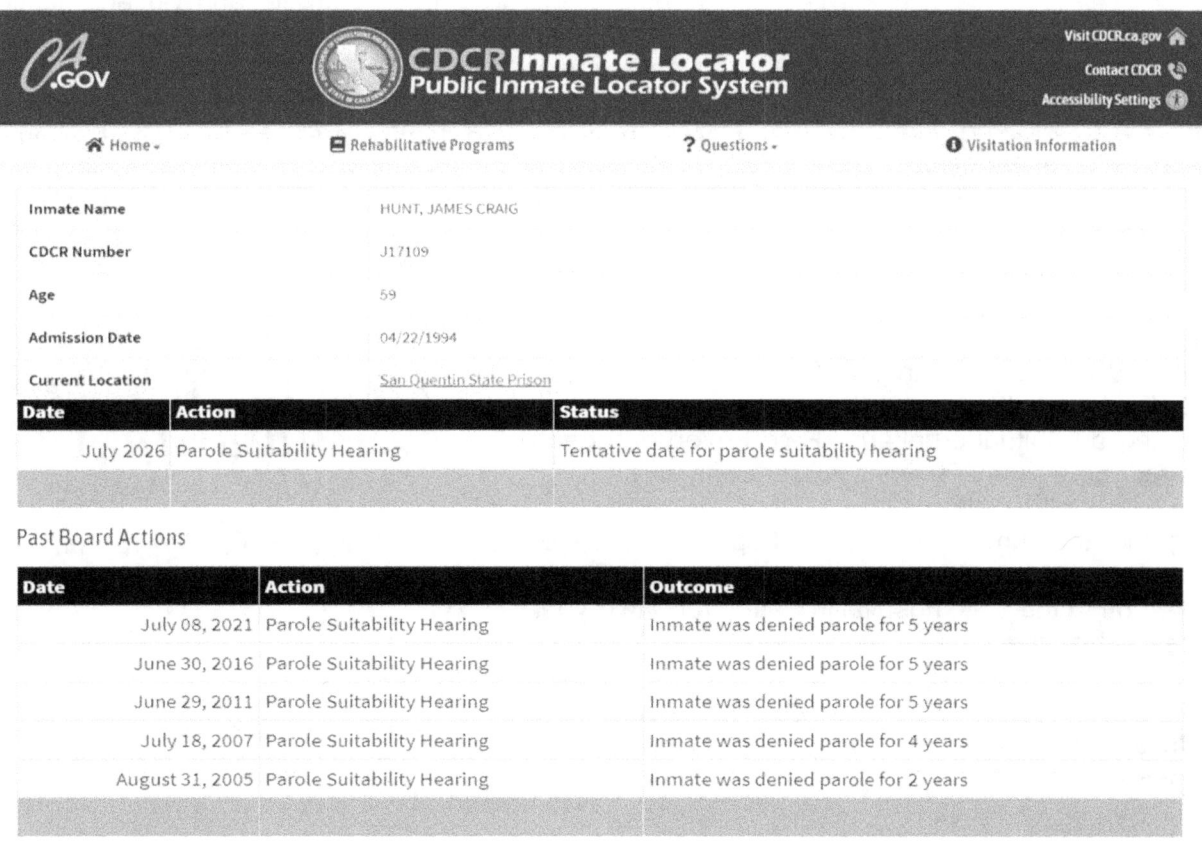

Leopoldo Ramiro "Joe" Foxen

Joe Foxen shot and killed Clorinda Gutierrez on November 4, 1912. Leaving parochial school with a bevy of friends, the 16-year-old girl was deliberately shot down by the 17-year-old rejected suitor, Foxen. Jealousy was cited by prosecutors as the motive for the murder. It was commented that she had recently refused to dance with Foxen and had accepted his rival's invitation at a party a few evenings ago.

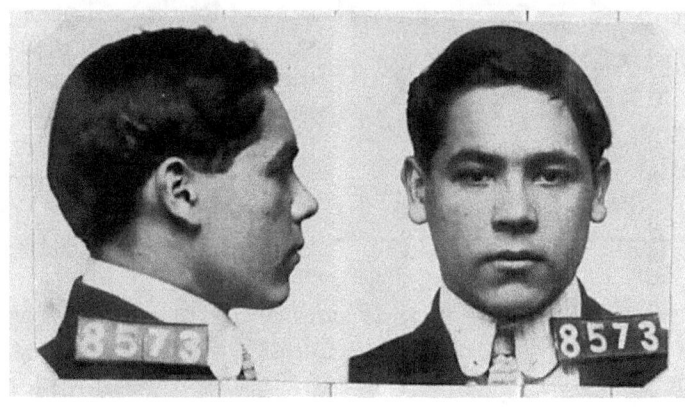

Gutierrez died at St. Francis hospital in Santa Barbara due to the gunshot wound inflicted by Foxen as he awaited her after school. Only recently paroled from juvenile incarceration, Foxen, who pleaded not guilty, had no good reputation to stand on.

Defense for this school yard murder rested on mental defect. There was much outrage, and vigilante justice was threatened in the form of a local posse insisting that "lynching" was too good for such as him.

Wanting to avoid a death penalty at any cost, the family bared its soul to the entire community, pointing to a terrible childhood and a lack of mental stability as extenuating circumstances. The elder Foxen faced the court in his son's defense.

Loyal.

PARENTS BARE THE SKELETON.

SANTA BARBARA SLAYER SUPPORTED BY HIS FAMILY.

Father Admits that He Is and Has Always Been a Heavy Drinker and that Son Was Literally Born in Alcohol and Had Never Been Normal.

Epifanio "Pete" Foxen, father of "Joe" went before the court and Judge Crow in an effort to show why he, himself, shouldn't be committed to the insane asylum for being a habitual drunkard. Pete Foxen had been arrested more than 200 times in fourteen years.

Altogether the sum of events added up to the younger Foxen being given a life sentence and the elder Foxen packed off to the state hospital in Patton for a two-year course of treatment.

Then, as today, life seldom means life. Twenty-one years later, the younger Foxen was given a chance at a redeemed life.

Convict Sentenced As Youth, Released In Maturity At 39

FOLSOM PRISON, April 26, (LP) — Twenty-one years after prison gates closed on an 18-year-old boy, they opened today for Leopoldo Foxen, of Santa Barbara, now 39.

Foxen, convicted of killing his sweetheart, Clorinda Guiterrez, in a jealous rage, was released on parole to permit him to go to New York where he has been promised employment.

John Logan "Buddy" Spears

Death struck two Santa Maria families when a young husband fatally shot and killed his wife and then took his own life leaving an infant daughter orphaned.

It was September 1944, and high school sweethearts Buddy Spears and Ruby Lucille Loring, once popular and well-known students at Santa Maria High, were dead in an unexplainable tragedy.

Spears learned the shoemaker's trade under Harry Takken of Santa Maria and opened a shop of his own in Lompoc. He married the former Miss Loring after her graduation on June 6, 1941. He sold the business two years later after suffering a nervous breakdown. He joined the Navy but was discharged after a number of months.

Reportedly despondent, morose and moody, Spears wrote a note to his young wife telling her that he intended to commit suicide. On finding the note, Ruby Spears sought out her husband in a desperate attempt to dissuade him. He had been out of sorts since his discharge from the Navy some months ago. Ruby Spears found him on the back steps of

their cottage. It is unclear if the two wrestled with the gun resulting in the wife's death or if Spears shot her intentionally before turning the gun on himself in a desperate murder-suicide.

The families buried them side to side in the Santa Maria Cemetery.

Ruby Loring Weds John Spears in Simple Rites

Miss Ruby Loring, a member of this year's graduating class of the high school, and John Spears, who escorted her to the class banquet and the junior prom last night, took "time out" between the banquet and the prom to be married at a simple certmony in the home of her parents, Mr. and Mrs. James Loring, 625 South Lincoln.

The bride wore her "prom" dress of white net. Her flowers were white gardenias. She was attended by Miss Beth Slater of San Luis Obispo, who wore robin's egg blue taffeta, with baby orchids. Oscar Reiner Jr. was best man.

The Rev. A. C. Bussingham, vicar of St. Peter's Episcopal church, read the wedding ceremony, before an improvised altar in a room decorated with Cecil Bruner roses and daisies and lighted by candlelight. Only members of the immediate families, and a few intimate friends of the couple, attended.

When the bridal pair appeared at the "prom," the orchestra struck up "Here Comes the Bride," word having "got around" that the marriage was taking place.

Young friends of the couple went to the home of the bridegroom's parents, Mr. and Mrs. Ralph Spears, for a brief reception after the "prom." The newlyweds left immediately afterward for their new home in Lompoc, and will leave late today for a short wedding trip. Young Spears has established a business in Lompoc.

Chapter 4: Suicide-Self Murder

Suicide is a leading cause of death. There are many perspectives on self-murder. It is basically defined as when someone injures themselves to the extent that they die. Suicide is not a simple subject to explore. There are many victims in a suicide case. Suicide has been considered everything from a crime to a sin, to mental illness or temporary insanity. It is the permanent solution to a temporary problem. Different societies treat it in different ways.

Murad Jacob "Jack" Kevorkian
(May 26, 1928 – June 3, 2011)

> Frank Scott, a young farmer of Santa Maria, committed suicide Christmas morning by shooting himself in the back of the head with his revolver. The coroner's jury yesterday afternoon brought in a verdict in accordance with the facts of the case. The suicide was but 27 years old, a native of the valley, and generally regarded as a "hard character."

Jack Kevorkian was an American pathologist. He promoted euthanasia as a humane choice for terminally ill people. He publicly championed a terminal patient's right to die quietly and comfortably with physician-assisted suicide. He claimed, "Dying is not a crime." Kevorkian claimed that he assisted at least 130 patients to death.

In 1998, Kevorkian was arrested and tried for his direct responsibility in the case of voluntary euthanasia on a man named Thomas Youk, 52, who suffered from Lou Gehrig's disease, or amyotrophic lateral sclerosis. Kevorkian was convicted of second-degree murder and served eight years of a 10-to-25 year sentence. He was released on parole on June 1, 2007, on condition that he would not offer advice about, participate in, or be present at the act of any type of suicide involving euthanasia to any other person, as well as neither promote nor talk about the procedure of assisted suicide.

His conviction led to him being dubbed in the media with the name "Dr. Death." While there was outcry that what he did was a crime, there was also support for his perspective. Not all death is worth postponing.

Typically, state law distinguishes between euthanasia and the withdrawing life support. Under very rigid requirements, euthanasia is legal in California since 2015.

Today, there are humane choices to ease from live to death. Who hasn't seen the morphine button that is provided in hospice settings? However, while we quietly dispense euthanasia to the elderly, we are not always prepared to give in to debilitating disease or withhold heroic measures for the young.

Suicide is always a headline. It's not rare or new; we are all familiar with Cleopatra committing suicide with an asp following the death of Mark Antony in 30 BC! There is, however, a certain macabre fascination about the process in the case of young, healthy people who choose to not go on with their lives. Rarely do families find peace or understanding with the decision. It is most defiantly the permanent solution to temporary problems. Great effort has been placed towards suicide prevention.

A few Santa Maria Times headlines, 1900-1910

LOUIS ARELLANES DIED BY HIS OWN HAND WEDNESDAY

No Reason Given For Rash Act

R. M. RIGHETTI OF SAN LUIS COMMITTS SUICIDE SUNDAY

Sunday evening, R. M. Righetti, of the firm of Tognazzini & Righetti, of San Luis Obispo, committed suicide by shooting himself. Ill health is said to have been the cause. The deceased was 38 years of age and leaves a wife, and two sons, besides several brothers. Frank Righetti of Guadalupe was a brother.

Chuichi Miyoshi, aged 30 years and 11 months committed suicide on Wednesday by strychnine poisoning.

O. D. Shorb attempted to commit suicide on Thursday afternoon with a 25-calibre automatic pistol. He shot himself above the heart and according to the latest reports will recover.

SUICIDE NOTE LEFT AT THE INN

Leaving a note telling of his decision to "quit this world," Jas. Kohout, house man at the Santa Maria Inn, disappeared this morning. Kohout had been at the Inn about a month. He was born in Austria but said he was an American citizen. Lately, according to Charles Reed, the proprietor of the Inn, Kohout had been brooding over the fact that he had been accused falsely of being a pro-German. He had worked in the ship yards at Seattle but left there when he had trouble with the other workers who called him an alien enemy.

Those who knew him said he showed no signs of insanity other than that he was suffering from "dementia praecox" in imagining that people were accusing him. A thorough search is being made for the man. The note he left to Mr. Reed said: "When you read this I will have passed from this life as this strain is more than I can stand. I have been accused unjustly of saying things that I did not utter. What one says can be construed by anyone evil enough to so construe the remark. Well, maybe they will also be judged. I know that God has helped me to bear up in this trouble. Thanking you all for your kindness." James Kohout.

SANTA BARBARA COUNTY.

Robert Brierly, an aged pioneer of Lompoc, committed suicide by cutting his throat with a knife. No other cause is known for the deed than that he had become despondent over financial embarrassments and in a fit of temporary insanity, brought on by heavy drinking, cut his throat.

Suicide of Robert Braun.

Last Monday, July 30th, while in a fit of despondency, Robert Braun sent a bullet through his heart, and died instantly.

Robert Braun was a familiar figure on Santa Maria streets for a number of years, and at one time was a wealthy man. In the early days, before the town was anything more than a cross roads camping place, Robert was a highly respected, honest and industrous blacksmith, and by frugality he amassed a considerable property. But the old story tells his tale. Adversity, then drink, with the inevitable finale.

With his property all wasted away, fair means or foul, broken in health, an old man, there was no open place for him to earn an honest living, and after being repulsed when asking for work at the asphalt mines at Sisquoc, he wandered a few rods from their office and sought the oblivion of the tomb.

A coroners jury empaneled soon learned the facts and were about to bury him in the Los Alamos potter's field when a number of the Masonic fraternity of which at one time he had been a member, ordered him decently dressed and buried and the bill sent them.

He leaves a widow, from whom he had been separated a number of years, but no children.

May his soul rest in peace.

Robert Braun

Lay him away in a pauper's grave,
  His friends have forsaken him now,
No one cares to bid him farewell
  Nor to tenderly stroke his brow;
Ah, worldly friendship is but a farce
  To those who misfortune keeps down,
He sought for friends and he sought in vain,
  For the friendship that does not abound
No one cares for the good he did
  In the years that have long since flown,
When he welcomed them, the hungry and poor,
  Though it were but a dog, to his home;
But God remembers the kindness done
  By the low as well as the high,
And he will welcome poor Robert Braun,
  To his home beyond the sky.   —L.

Ross Leonard (Scott) Galyon

Police investigated the suicide of Ross L. Galyon, age 22, on March 26, 1948. He was a World War II veteran, married and lived at 112-A Camino Colegio. His body was reported by Mrs. Kay Berreyessa who was making her home with the young couple. It was reported that Galyon came home around 9 p.m., laid down on the bed and fired a .32 caliber bullet into his head above and to the front of his right ear. The weapon was identified as a French FNH pistol, standard Nazi side arm issue, probably a war trophy.

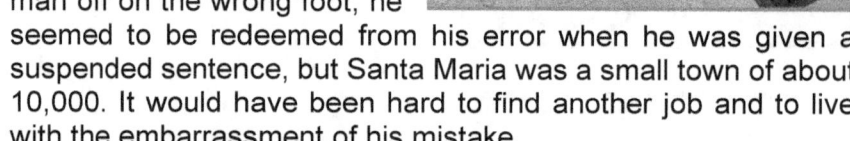

Galyon had created some trouble for himself when he was convicted of embezzlement August, 1946. A young married man off on the wrong foot, he seemed to be redeemed from his error when he was given a suspended sentence, but Santa Maria was a small town of about 10,000. It would have been hard to find another job and to live with the embarrassment of his mistake.

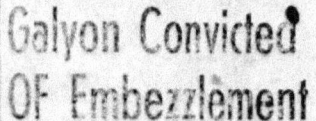

Galyon Convicted OF Embezzlement

Ross Leonard Galyon, 21, of Santa Maria, was convicted of four counts of embezzlement by a Federal District Court jury in Los Angeles yesterday.

Galyon was charged with the embezzlement of $1950 from the local branch of the Bank of America while in their employe for a brief period last Spring.

The case was referred to probation authorities for review, and sentence will be handed down Friday, Aug. 30, in the Los Angeles court.

Galyon Receives Suspended Sentence

Ross Leonard Galyon, 21, of Santa Maria, convicted on four counts of embezzlement by a Federal District Court jury, yesterday was given a three-year suspended sentence and placed on probation by Judge Campbell Beaumont of Los Angeles.

Galyon's suicide, like all suicides, is hard to understand. When a person commits suicide, the whole family feels indicted. His wife, Marjorie F. Galyon, who was away at the time he took his own life, would have been lain with a great burden. She couldn't know that lightening was going to strike her twice.

Robert Patrick Foxen

Bride-elect Is Shower Guest

Miss Marge Galyon, whose marriage to Robert Foxen will take place this summer, was complimented at a gift shower in the home of Mrs. Arthur Simas, Newlove drive, on Tuesday.

A blue and white color scheme was carried out. Under a blue and white umbrella tied to a chandelier was placed the table, on which guests deposited miscellaneous gifts as they arrived.

A grand wedding was about to take place. It was 1950, and Mr. and Mrs. Robert Patrick Foxen were planning to make their home in Pasadena. The bride was the former Marjorie Felicity Galyon, daughter of Mr. and Mrs. T. Moore of Santa Maria and the wife of Ross L. Galyon, above. The bridegroom was the son of Mr. and Mrs. E.E. Foxen, 625 S. Lincoln, members of a pioneer family of Santa Barbara County. An approximate 100 guests would attend the wedding. Robert Patrick Foxen served in the United States Navy and the Coast Guard during World War II. Lately, he attended barber's college.

July 8, 1957, it was reported that a 36-year-old oilfield worker strangled himself in his bedroom the previous day. It was Robert Patrick Foxen. Authorities ruled the death at 410 W.

Marjorie Felicity Moore Sweeney Galyon Foxen Brown Lawrence Brooker, c. 1950

Chapel St. suicide. The motive given was that Foxen had received divorce papers from his wife, Margie in Mexico. Mrs. Jennie Dwyer, a neighbor discovered his body.

The circumstances of death were not ordinary. Foxen was found with a leather collar around his neck. The collar was attached to a rope suspended from a hook in the door frame of a closet. His arms and ankles were pulled in back of his body by slings attached to other hooks in the door frame. He was drawn into a kneeling position above a stack of magazines on the floor of his bedroom.

Marjorie Foxen was the former Marjorie F. Moore. In 1943 she was known as Margie Felicity Sweeney and in 1946 as Marjorie T. Galyon. After Mr. Foxen's death in 1957, she remarried and became Marjorie Brown, then in July 1960 she was Marjorie Lawrence, married to David E. Lawrence of Sacramento. In 1969 she was known as Margie Felicity Brooker. Born 13 February 1921 in Sacramento, California, Margie had at least six husbands before her passing in December 19, 2001.

Robert Patrick Foxen

Floyd Sutherland Teachout

TEACHOUT ENDS LIFE WITH ROPE NEAR HIGHWAY

Former Santa Marian Kills Himself Returning Home From Visit Here

Floyd Sutherland Teachout, 31, a former Santa Maria resident ended his own life, Thursday night, March 31, 1938. He pulled his automobile off the road at San Marcos pass and hanged himself from a tree a few hundred feet off the road. There is no indication why he chose to commit suicide. There was more than eight dollars in his pocket and no sign of trouble in or around the site where his body was discovered some 10-12 hours after he died at his own hand.

Teachout had been amiably visiting with friends earlier in the day and seemed in good humor. His death, although not suspicious, certainly seems without reason.

Santa Maria Woman Attempts Suicide

Death by suicide isn't as easy to accomplish as many believe. A Santa Maria woman failed to end her life when a 'bullet' from a small gun failed to penetrate her forehead. The 28-year-old woman, whose name is not disclosed, attempted suicide in a local hotel room early this morning police reported to the *Santa Maria Times* on August 2, 1952.

She had attempt to shoot herself through the head with what officers referred to as a 'pellet' gun. With the bullet lodged in her head, the women called a cab. Police arrived and took her to Sisters hospital for removal of the pellet then took her to the Santa Maria hospital for evaluation on "hold" orders. She was booked in city jail at 12:50 a.m. today.

Filippo Frusconi Rusconi

In August 1966, Filippo Rusconi, 80, of 320 W. Alvin Street, was found hanging from a fruit tree outside his home. The county coroner's office called his death a suicide. Mr. Rusconi, a native of Switzerland, had been a farmer and a dairyman and had operated a local restaurant in Santa Maria for more than 22 years. The café became headline news in January 1945 when a P-38 crashed into it killing three people, including his wife, Demotilda Rusconi. Rusconi remarried and rebuilt from that tragedy.

Suicide is a door once opened that can be contagious. In August 1998, Phillip "Fausto" Rusconi, son of Filippo, committed suicide at the home.

Amityville Horror House, site of a family murder supposed to have been satanically inspired. For Sale!

Does a Violent Death in a House have to be Disclosed?

A lot of states require homeowners and, by extension, their real estate agents to disclose certain information about the properties they list for sale. A majority of these disclosures revolve around the physical condition of the property. California has recognized that certain intangible facts such as a violent death, suicide or brutal crime could affect the property's desirability and thus its value. It is generally agreed that a residence where a violent crime has occurred should have the incident disclosed to perspective buyers. The overall value of the home may be directly impacted. The California Civil Code requires disclosure of deaths at a property listed for sale when the death occurred within the last three years and was not AIDS related.

The National Association of Realtors (NAR) defines a property as a stigmatized property when it has been "psychologically impacted by an event, which occurred or was suspected to have occurred on or within the property or boundaries of the property. Examples of stigmatizing factors include murder, suicide and other deaths, serious crime, proximity to registered sex offenders, hauntings and other paranormal activity. According to NAR, "only 15 percent of potential homebuyers would pay full market value for an impacted home. A further 19 percent would expect a 31 to 50 percent discount for purchasing such a property."

State law does not release the home seller from his duty of honesty. In most states, if the buyer asks a specific question about past macabre happenings, the seller is legally compelled to tell the truth about the event. This remains true even if the potential buyer's question requires an answer that exceeds the three-year disclosure requirements set. Courts are increasingly holding stigma-type defects to the same disclosure standards as physical defects.

Here is a short list of some hard to turn real estate due to crime. The Ramsey House, Boulder Colorado, site of the murder of little beauty queen Jon Benet Ramsey, the Lee Harvey Oswald Rooming House in Dallas Texas home to assassin of President John F. Kennedy, Chi Omega Sorority House, Tallahassee, Florida, scene of Ted Bundy's rampage. "In Cold Blood House," Holcomb Kansas site of Truman Capote's novel and them murder of the Herb Clutter family and the Lizzie Borden House, Fall River Massachusetts, where she took an ax and gave her parent 40 whacks!

Chapter 5: Unsolved Cases-Cold Cases

The Black Dahlia

Some cases are destined from the moment of discovery to be infamous. While today we are used to serial killers being given media worthy names, the murder of Elizabeth Short was a standout in its timeline. It was a dramatic, heinous event, the first of its kind post World War II.

The Black Dahlia is one of Hollywood's most famous unsolved murder cases. It unfolded when the raven-haired, 22-year-old Elizabeth Short was found murdered on Norton Avenue between 39th and Coliseum streets in Los Angeles. On the morning of January 15, 1947, a mother taking her child for a walk in a Los Angeles neighborhood stumbled upon a gruesome sight: the body of a young naked woman.

The body was just a few feet from the sidewalk and posed in such a way that the mother reportedly thought it was a mannequin at first glance. Her body had been cut in half at the waist and appeared to have been drained of all blood with the precision of an expert. Despite the extensive mutilation and cuts on the body, there wasn't a drop of blood at the scene, indicating that the young woman had been killed elsewhere. The killer had also cut 3-inch gashes into each corner of her mouth, creating a spooky, clown-like grin. Today we would call it, the Joker smile. Marks on her body suggested the woman had been bound and tortured, and her official cause of death was cerebral hemorrhage and shock.

> Police, previously convinced that a woman was responsible, widened their search after hearing Miss Smith's story and finding other clues which pointed to a man.

In a bizarre twist, police originally suspected a woman may have committed this crime against "Beautiful Beth."

The ensuing investigation was led by the Los Angeles Police Department. The FBI was asked to help, and it quickly identified the body—just 56 minutes after getting blurred fingerprints via a new technology "Soundphoto," a primitive facsimile machine used by news services. This was the first time in which this equipment was used by law enforcement to identify a victim.

Short's murder quickly became a sensation, not only because of its location in the "show biz" capital, but also because the police acted in tandem with the media to disseminate clues in hopes of discovering a prime suspect. Several people confessed, only to be later released for lack of evidence. Much speculation surrounded the details of Short's life. It is commonly held that Short was an aspiring actress, though she had no known acting credits or jobs during her time in Los Angeles. The LAPD began an extensive investigation that created over 150 suspects but produced no arrests.

Los Angeles Times
BLACK DAHLIA: *The Elizabeth Short murder case is reexamined on "48 Hours*

Elizabeth Short was born July 29, 1924, in Boston, Massachusetts, the third of five daughters of Cleo A. Short and wife Phoebe Mae Sawyer. In 1927, the Short family moved to Portland, Maine, briefly before settling in Medford (a Boston suburb) that same year. Short was raised and spent most of her life there. Short's father built miniature golf courses until the 1929 stock market crash when he lost most of his savings and the family became broke. In 1930, her father's car was found abandoned on the Charlestown Bridge, and it was presumed that he had committed suicide by jumping into the Charles River. Believing her husband dead, Short's mother moved with her five daughters into a small apartment in Medford and worked as a bookkeeper to support them. In actuality, Mr. Short had abandoned the responsibilities of his family and relocated to California.

Troubled by severe bronchitis and asthma attacks, Short underwent lung surgery at age 15. Doctors suggested she relocate to a milder climate during the winter months to ease her respiratory problems. Short's mother sent her to spend winters in Miami, Florida, with family friends. During the next three years, Short lived in Florida during the winter months and spent the rest of the year in Medford with her mother and sisters. In her sophomore year, Short dropped out of Medford High School.

In late 1942, Short's mother received a letter of apology from her presumed-deceased husband, which revealed that he was in fact alive and had started a new life. In December, at age 18, Short relocated to Vallejo to live with her father, whom she had not seen since she was six years old. At the time, he was working at the nearby Mare Island Naval Shipyard on San Francisco Bay. Arguments between Short and her father led to her moving out in January 1943.

'Camp Cooke Cutie'
The Feb. 26, 1943, issue of The Camp Cooke Clarion, weekly camp newspaper, carried a large photograph of Miss Short as the week's selection as "Camp Cooke Cutie," a weekly feature in the paper.
In a cut line on the photo, Miss Short was described as "beauteous Boston Beth... has been in camp just one month... is 18 years of age, five feet, five inches tall, weighs 125 pounds... likes dancing, ice skating, and horseback riding..."

She accepted a job at the Base Exchange at Camp Cooke (Vandenberg Air Force Base), near Santa Maria, living with several friends, and briefly with an Army Air Force sergeant who reportedly

The identity of a former Camp Cooke "buck" sergeant with whom Miss Short allegedly lived in Santa Maria as man and wife for a time in the late spring and early summer of 1943 is still unknown.

abused her. Short left in mid-1943 and moved to Santa Barbara, where she was arrested on September 23, 1943, for underage drinking at a local bar. The juvenile authorities sent her home to Medford, but she headed to Florida instead.

While in Florida, Short met Major Matthew Michael Gordon, Jr., a decorated Army Air Force officer at the 2nd Air Commando Group. He was training for deployment to the China Burma India Theater of Operations of World War II. Short told friends that Gordon had written to propose marriage while he was recovering from injuries from a plane crash in India. She accepted his offer, but Gordon died in a second crash on August 10, 1945, less than a week before the surrender of Japan ended the war.

Doubt If Wed to Air Hero

Pueblo, Colo., Jan. 18. (AP)—Mrs. Matt M. Gordon, sr., of Pueblo said tonight she did not believe her war hero son, Matt M. Gordon, jr., killed in an airplane crash in India in 1945, had ever married Elizabeth Short, whose nude and mutilated body was found in Los Angeles.

Mrs. Gordon said her son met Elizabeth in Miami in 1944, after his return from China where as a pilot he won the Air Medal and 15 Oak Leaf Clusters, the Distinguished Flying Cross and the Silver and Bronze Stars.

When Maj. Gordon left the States for India, he corresponded with Elizabeth, Mrs. Gordon said. She said she had sent a wire to Elizabeth Aug. 22 informing her of her son's death.

Returning to Los Angeles in July 1946, she visited Army Air Force Lieutenant Joseph Gordon Fickling, whom she had known from Florida. Fickling was stationed at the Naval Reserve Air Base in Long Beach. Short spent the last six months of her life in southern California, mostly in the Los Angeles area. Shortly before her death, she had been working as a waitress and rented a room behind the Florentine Gardens nightclub on Hollywood Boulevard. Grieving Gordon's tragic death at the close of the war, she reportedly befriended many men while frequenting jazz clubs making it nearly impossible to pin down one person she could have been with before she died. She acquired the nickname of the Black Dahlia posthumously. The owner of a drugstore in Long Beach, California, told reporters that male customers had that name for her. Short's reputation took a bit of a beating in the media. She was most assuredly a free spirit who sought out adventure and enjoyed a lot of freedoms not generally accorded women in the late 40s.

Joseph Gordon Fickling

The Family

Mother in California

The mother of Miss Short flew here today from Boston to give police what assistance she could in the hunt for the girl's fiendish slayer.

Mrs. Phoebe Mae Short, the mother, stopped here for 55 minutes before boarding a plane for Berkeley, where she will bring another daughter, Mrs. Virginia West, to be at the inquest.

Mrs. Short told newsmen that Elizabeth left home when she was a high school sophomore "to venture on her own."

Los Angeles Times SAT., JANUARY 18, 1947—Part I 3

SLAIN GIRL'S MOTHER DUE HERE TODAY FROM EAST

VICTIM'S KINFOLK—Mrs. Phoebe M. Short, 46, extreme left, mother of slain girl, shown on way to friend's home in Medford, Mass., with three other daughters— Dorothea, 24; Eleanor and Muriel, 18. Mrs. Short is scheduled to arrive here by plane today from Boston. Elizabeth's father Cleo yesterday was found living here.

The Friends

GIRLS WHO KNEW MURDERED BEAUTY AID POLICE

 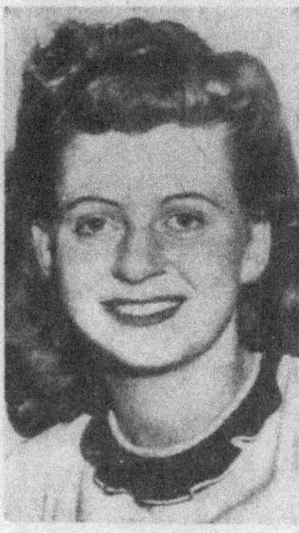 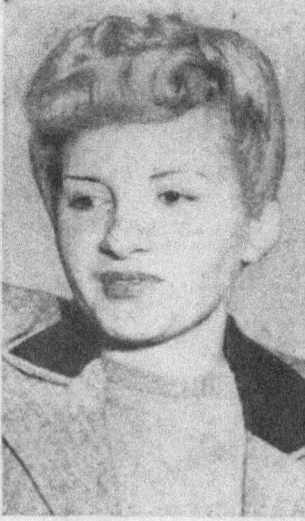 

FRIEND—Anne Toth, film bit player, said Elizabeth Short wired her for money from San Diego last month.

DEPARTS—Marjorie Graham returned East, but Elizabeth couldn't stand weather there, stayed here.

REPORTS—Linda Rohr said she lived in same apartment with Elizabeth, who "liked to prowl on the boulevard."

HOSTESS—Dorothy French said Elizabeth left San Diego Jan. 7 for Hollywood with unidentified red-haired boy.

Betty Short may not have been a movie star but she was well known and enjoyed a lot of the same kinds of notoriety as one. She had many friends and dated multiple men at once. From November 13 to December 5, Short resided in an apartment at 1842 N. Cherokee Street in Hollywood with a number of young women. Eight young women each paid $1 a day to rent the apartment. She was known as the girl with a different boyfriend every night. Linda Rohr, "She was always going out, and she loved to prowl the boulevard." Rohr, also 22, was a rouge-room worker at the Max Factor make-up studio. There was plenty of turnover. Only Sherryl Maylond, a cocktail lounge employee, and Marion Schmidt, a telephone operator, remained of the group who were Short's roommates. Others had moved and their double-decked bunks in the crowded double apartment had been filled by newcomers who never met Short.

Recalls Elderly Man

Miss Maylond recalled "a tall, sinister, elderly man" who approached her at the bar where she works a week ago and asked about Miss Short's whereabouts.

Others remembered that the slain girl had spoken frequently of a radio announcer named "Maurice" with a cultivated British accent.

The apartment manager, Mrs. Juanita Ringo, said Miss Short eluded her by a side door when she asked for rent last December. Mrs. Ringo held a suitcase which Miss Short reclaimed a few days later, paying her rent.

One roommate said Miss Short had asked her to accompany her to a Crescent Drive apartment in Beverly Hills, where a man would pay the rent. Another said she talked of moving to San Bernardino to work there at a military base.

The Suspects

After her death, she would forever be known as the Black Dahlia. It is hard to accept that there were men and women who confessed to the crime just to be linked with her. Others disappeared trying to obscure their connection. An aspiring actress or young women who used her beauty to get men to buy and provide for her while living large at their expense? Who was she really?

Suspect Hunted for Slaying of Elizabeth Short

Former Laramie Cowboy and Cook Is Released After Quizzing on Coast Case.

Los Angeles, Jan. 18. (AP)—Police pressed their search tonight for a red-haired man as the principal suspect in the butcher slaying of attractive, 22 year old Elizabeth Short, after releasing one of two men taken into custody earlier for questioning.

In Merced, Calif., Edward Glen Thorpe, Los Angeles cowboy, was released after questioning which Police Capt. Malon Stanley said disclosed Thorpe had nothing to do with the case.

More than 50 men and women went to the LAPD claiming to be the killer. These confessions made it extremely difficult for police. There were numerous more suspects throughout the years, but there was never enough evidence to charge anyone. There were multiple theories on the murder and how it could have been linked to other murders. Some detectives believed that the same person who committed the Cleveland Torso Murders also killed Elizabeth Short. Another viable theory at the time was that Short's murder was linked to the Lipstick murders. Many believed the main reason that the murder was unsolved was because of the media's interference and meddling. Officers and detectives stated that reporters were walking over evidence and withholding information that they received from callers to their offices. At one point the reporters were in the LAPD station and were just freely answering phones that could've have been tips for the investigation and withholding that information.

Daniel S. Voorhees (left) told Los Angeles police he killed Elizabeth Short—but detectives yesterday discredited his "confession." Shown with Voorhees are Detective Al Shambra (center) and Booking Officer Charles Pascoe. (AP wirephoto)

Cecil French, 23, of Bakersfield, questioned after he was picked up for assertedly molesting women at Sixth and Los Angeles Sts., was freed from City Jail and eliminated from the case.

The case has become one of the most famous unsolved murders in the world. Generations of law enforcement have looked for ways to solve this crime. An account was written by Steve Hodel who implicated his own father, a Los Angeles doctor, as the Black Dahlia murderer. Most recently British writer Piu Eatwell's wrote her theory centered on Leslie Duane Dillon, a bellhop and one-time mortician's assistant who was briefly considered the case's primary suspect, before police let him go. She writes that the LAPD knowingly let Short's murderer off the hook because Sergeant Finis Brown, one of the case's two lead investigators, was an alleged corrupt cop with links to Mark Hansen, a local nightclub and movie theater owner and Leslie Dillon's purported co-conspirator in Short's death. She published her solution to the crime in a book she titled, *Black Dahlia, Red Rose*. Hansen died of natural causes in 1964. No charges were ever brought against him. He had no criminal record and no known history of violence.

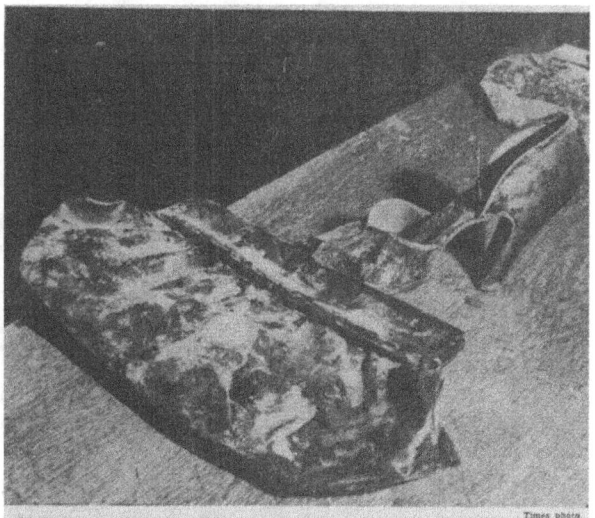

SHOE AND BAG IDENTIFIED—Bag carried by Elizabeth Short and a shoe she wore, shown with light dusting of ashes, were identified yesterday by Robert (Red) Manley, who brought her here from San Diego and left her at hotel six days before slaying.

LAPD Police Chief William Worton said there was absolutely no case against Hansen. Popular accounts of the Black Dahlia case often portray Hansen as having connections to organized crime, but there is no evidence of this either according to records everyone from "queer woman surgeon" to Bugsy Siegel has been named as a possible perpetrator! No charges were ever filed and the case was never closed. This case remains the longest running open case of the LAPD.

At Rest

In loving memory
ELIZABETH "BETTY" SHORT
July 29, 1924 - January 15, 1947
We have looked beyond earth's shadows and sought the truth with strengthened will.

Death notice in a Los Angeles newspaper

Epilogue-Santa Maria Connection

Bruno Zemaitis was involved in the investigation when it was felt that someone from Santa Maria could possibly have been involved in the crime. According to the records of Zemaitis, Short had spent considerable time at the Snappy Lunch Diner, located at the corner of Broadway and Cook streets in Santa Maria. According to Bruno's wife, Beth who worked at Snappy Lunch at the time, the woman had shoulder-length jet black hair, the color of which was set off by the red flower that she always wore. She was a beauty; everyone would stop talking whenever she walked in the door. Her alabaster skin color and her light blue eyes contrasted with her black hair.

Wac on Way to Help

Word was received from Montgomery, Ala., that W.A.C. Sgt. Mary Stradder, with whom Miss Short reportedly lived at Casmalia near Santa Maria, at the time the victim worked in a Camp Cooke post exchange, will arrive here tomorrow to give what aid she can to the authorities, Donahoe reported.

Because of reported threats made by an Army supply sergeant with whom the "Black Dahlia" was said to have lived as man and wife in 1943, investigators were anxious to question Mrs. Stradder regarding the slain girl's activities at

J. Charles Collins

August, 1964, found stabbed to death in his own bed at 116 S. Vine Street, Charlie Collins was pronounced dead on the scene. Collins was an unemployed laborer at the time of his death. He was killed by a single knife stab that penetrated the heart while he slept at his small two-room house behind Anne's Beauty Shop on the corner of Vine and Church Streets. Collins' body was discovered by a visitor, Frank Sounders, who came by around 8:30 a.m. An examination determined time of death to be between 4:30 to 5:30 a.m.

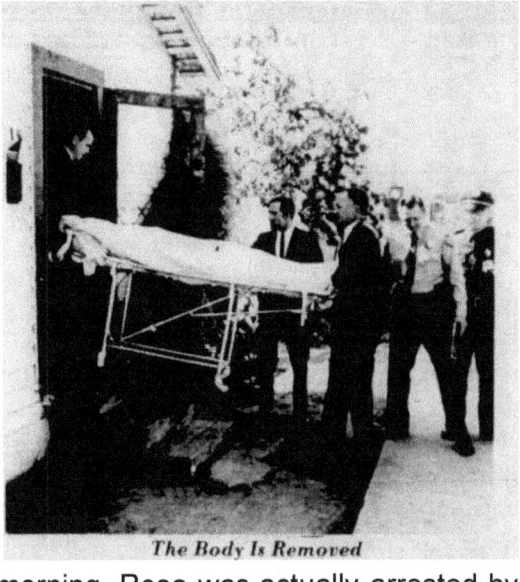

The Body Is Removed

Solemn Suspect

J. D. Rose, 37, was arrested. He was a milker for a local Santa Maria Dairy. The men had been drinking together into the early hours of the morning. Rose was actually arrested by California Highway Patrol for "drunk pedestrian in an auto" and given a 30-day sentence before the body was even discovered. Rose made a plea agreement for voluntary manslaughter, but it all fell apart as the accused was subjected to an illegal search of his property and his confession was attained without giving him right to council. Blood evidence was not admissible and the confession was not permitted to be introduced in court. The DA never further pursue this case, it remains open.

it was shown some of this evidence may have been collected from Rose's car without benefit of a search warrant. Also, length of time between Rose's arrest on a drunk charge that day and the time of the search of the automobile several hours later may cause the evidence to never be admitted or accepted.

The Case of Robert Lee Lopez

Fast forward to 1980

This headline chilled Santa Maria residents. Gang violence and activity seemed to be unrelenting. Shootings and knifings dominated the headlines. Much of the violence occurred between young Hispanic males. Street fights with chains and bullets raining out on young men standing curbside in their neighborhoods made the news. So many eyes on the violence, yet no witnesses to testify to the grim reality that was north Santa Maria. No one saw anything to report and no identifications get made.

Unsolved Santa Maria homicides total four over last eight months

Bobby Lopez was 20 years old when he was murdered on August the 18th, 1980 in Evans Park, north of Donovan Road, Santa Maria. It is estimated that at least 50 people were present when he was stabbed in the chest. No witness has ever spoken out for Bobby Lopez. Even a $50,000 reward didn't inspire a single eye witness to step forward and name Bobby's killer.

It was reported that this was a gang-related attack. With so many young adults in the area at the time who actually witnessed the stabbing, it is almost inconceivable that no one was of a mind to step forward and identify Bobby's killer and give him justice. Everyone present denied seeing anything when questioned by detectives and later by the grand jury.

A person of interest denied any involvement in the death. This one suspect remains free, largely because it is believed that the witnesses have been intimidated to the point that they fear for their own safety.

Cold case — The state offered a $50,000 reward in November for the 25-year-old unsolved murder of Robert "Bobby" Lopez, 20, who was fatally stabbed in August 1980. Police say they've long had a suspect but not enough evidence to make an arrest.

January 1, 2006

Robert Lee Lopez of West Monroe Street was found stabbed to death in the playground of the housing area at Evans Park. He was struck once with a large knife in the heart. The incident began about 4:52 a.m. when a report was telephoned to police of an unknown male victim lying on the ground near the swings at the playground.

The Santa Barbara County grand jury conducted a hearing at Santa Maria City Hall Wednesday regarding the stabbing death of Robert Lee Lopez, whose body was found Aug. 18 on the playground of the Evans Park housing project.

Police and district attorney's spokesmen are not revealing the identity of the suspect in the case, but The Times has learned that investigations have centered on Paul Gutierrez, a Santa Maria resident currently serving time in county jail on a petty theft conviction.

No action was taken by the grand jury at Wednesday's hearing, but the investigation into the death of Lopez, 21, is continuing, according to Santa Maria police.

This resident, who did not want to be identified, said another person had come to her home and told her about the body. She and her teenage son walked over to see the victim before contacting police. Lopez had been dead a short period of time. There was enough blood on scene for police to believe the stabbing occurred on that location. No weapon was found at the scene. Police did a door-to-door canvas of the area.

Lopez had been questioned by police only a few hours before in connection with an earlier incident at the Peppertree Plaza shopping center. He was with two girls when this occurred around 12:30 a.m. There had been a shooting incident at the plaza. Although the Bobby Lopez investigation reached a roadblock years ago, his family and the Santa Maria Police Department are still seeking justice.

Robert L. Lopez

Robert L. Lopez, 20, died Monday of a stab wound. He was born May 18, 1960, in Van Horn, Tex., and was a lifelong resident of Santa Maria. He attended Santa Maria High School.

Attempted murder charges dropped

Attempted murder charges against Paul Gutierrez, 22, and Roy Estrada, 21, both of Santa Maria have been temporarily dropped, according to Assistant District Attorney Larry Sutton.

The two were scheduled for arraignment in Municipal Court Tuesday, but Judge Robert G. Eckhoff "temporarily rejected" the case. Sutton said this morning that he has asked the police to further investigate the matter and provide more information. The charges will be refiled as soon as the information is on hand, he said.

Meanwhile, Gutierrez is scheduled to appear again in Superior Court today for a criminal readiness and settlement conference on a felony charge of possessing a pistol, a violation of probation for a robbery conviction he received earlier.

The two men were arrested Saturday and held on $100,000 bail for allegedly stabbing Michael Buelna in the 200 block of West Williams. Buelna was found sitting on his couch with a stab wound on his throat shortly after 2 a.m.

Gutierrez remained in custody due to his scheduled appearance in Superior Court, and Estrada is in custody on a California Youth Authority hold for past criminal activities.

Paul Aros Gutierrez, 21 was arrested August 21, three days after the stabbing of Bobby Lopez, for the burglary of a set of stereo speakers from a friend's car at The Hydrant, a bar at 409 S. Blosser, on August 19. He eventually pleaded guilty to petty theft and was convicted. Gutierrez' record also includes an arrest for armed robbery on December 4, 1976. He was charged with entering 7-11 store with a shotgun and robbing the cash register of $45 and two customers of their wallets. He plead guilty and was sentenced to the California Youth Authority. He was 17 at the time of the armed robbery. He would continue to have brushes with the law and gang violence. Gutierrez, now 62, is currently at the California Institution for Men. He was never charged in connection to Bobby Lopez's murder.

- The felony arrest Sunday of Paul Aros Gutierrez, 52, transient, on bench warrant, failure to appear, and misdemeanor giving false identification to peace officer, bench warrant, failure to appear. No bail.

- The felony arrest Tuesday of Paul Aros Gutierrez, 44, 500 block North L Street, on suspicion of possession of a narcotic controlled substance, willful cruelty to a child that is likely to cause great bodily injury, and misdemeanor counts of battery domestic violence and possession of a hypodermic needle or syringe. His bail was set at $30,000.

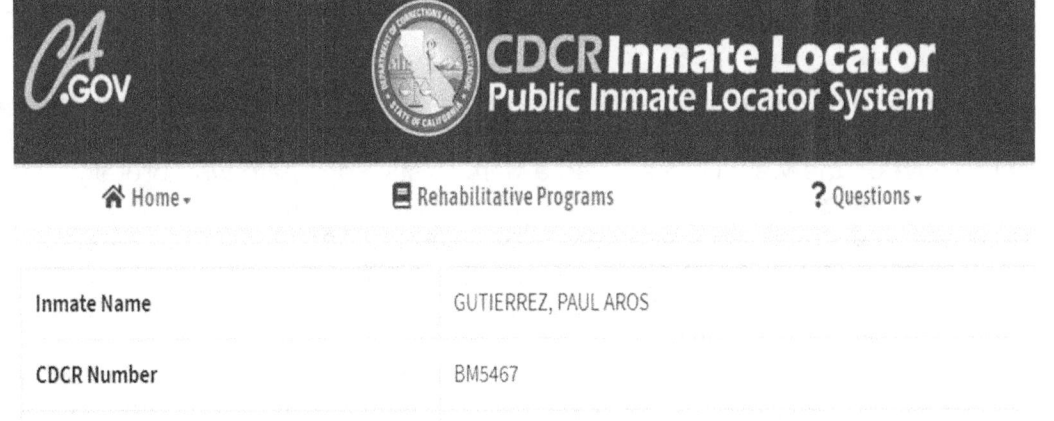

Inmate Name	GUTIERREZ, PAUL AROS
CDCR Number	BM5467
Age	62
Admission Date	11/19/2020
Current Location	California Institution for Men

Chapter 6: Cold Blooded Murder

When someone kills in cold blood, they murder in a way that is especially cruel, showing no emotion, displaying severe violence or extreme aggressive. The act may be punishing, or it may reflect a mental defect described as sociopathy. Ninety-nine percent of the population is not sociopaths. One percent is! Within that one percent, there are some that are so inhuman, so bone-chillingly scary, that they become famous. Unfortunately, that is exactly what they want, and their infamy excites them to such a degree that prison is just another playground for them to experiment in. Signs of the sociopath are: (1) lying, (2) irresponsibility, (3) manipulation, (4) lack of emotion. A sociopath is so dangerous because he or she is extremely charming, very personable, so persuasive that you want to believe them. They take you unsuspectingly into dangerous situations.

Not every sociopath is a serial killer. The trend is that the most brutal, violent killers are sociopaths. They are often labeled with media friendly names, like the "toolbox killer" or the "zodiac killer" and become infamous to their complete enjoyment. What follows are few names of some of the worst of the worst sociopaths.

John Wayne Gacy resided in Illinois. He was the "poster boy" of both local and national citizenship, received a Man of the Year award from his city's Junior Chamber of Commerce and, separately, had his picture taken with Rosalynn Carter, the First Lady of the United States. He performed for children as a clown at birthday parties, public gatherings and hospitals. He was adored and admired in his community. What wasn't known was that he was a sociopath. In fact, he became one of the most famous sociopaths to ever draw breath. In the 1970s, he tortured, raped and murdered thirty-three young men. He buried most of them in the crawl space under his house. Apprehended in 1980, the "Killer Clown" died by lethal injection May, 1994.

Ted Bundy was a good-looking, charismatic young man living in Seattle in the 1970s. He was referred to as "The Campus Killer." He lured women to him with his magnetic personality. Dozens fell prey and were brutally beaten, raped and murdered. He escaped suspicion for decades. It is estimated he had more than 30 victims over seven states. He was apprehended in August of 1976 and convicted. He sat on death row for nine years and was executed in the electric chair January of 1989.

Jeffrey MacDonald had power and respect as an Army Captain in the Green Berets and as a medical doctor at Fort Bragg, North Carolina. He was a husband, the father of two daughters with another child (boy) on the way. He was also a narcissistic sociopath who brutally murdered his pregnant wife and daughters and tried to blame "hippies." Convicted in 1970, he is currently serving three consecutive life sentences after being denied parole in 2021. He was sentenced without the possibility of parole but has appealed that repeatedly. He continues to maintain his innocence. He is sometimes known as the "Fatal Vision Killer."

Jeffrey Dahmer, the "Milwaukee Cannibal," raped, murdered, dismembered, and ate parts of his victims, seventeen boys and men in the 70s and 80s. He drilled holes and injected Draino or hot water into their brains trying to "create" sex zombies. He was apprehended in 1991 and sentenced to 15 terms of life imprisonment. In 1994, Dahmer was beaten to death by a fellow inmate, Christopher Scarver. Scarver divulged why he brutally murdered him. "Some people who are in prison are repentant, but he was not one of them." Dahmer used to fashion limbs out of the

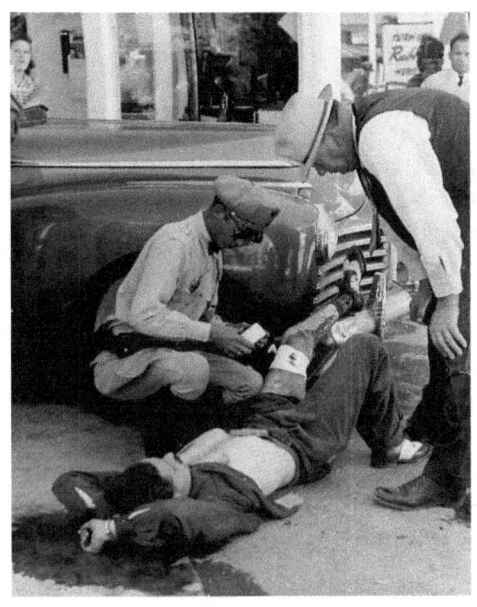

prison food, applying ketchup on places to represent blood, acting out his 'cannibal' behavior. Scarver took a metal bar and crushed his skull. Dahmer preyed on gay, black men.

Diane Downs was 'in love' with a man who didn't want children, and she was the mother of three. To get her man, she shot her own young children. She was called the "Mommy Murderess." She was sentenced in June of 1984 to life + 50 with the possibility of parole after 25 years. She escaped once and an additional 5 years was added to her sentence. She has been denied parole three times but maintains her innocence. She has been eligible to apply for parole again since 2020. Two of the three children survived.

Life Term Convict Dies in State Prison

WAUPUN, Wis., July 5 (AP)—Robert Taylor Bailey, 23, serving a life term in the Wisconsin state penitentiary for the murder of two Kenosha social workers in 1942, died this morning in the prison hospital.

Warden Luke F. Murphy said Bailey had been ill since June 26 with what was described by prison authorities as "a mild brain infection."

Aileen Wuornos was abandoned as an infant by her mother to a child molesting father. Wuornos was pregnant at age 14. She worked as a prostitute and admitted to murdering seven men. She was known as the "Damsel of Death." She was given six death sentences. She was executed by lethal injection October 2002 at age 46.

Soldier Sought in Rape-Murder

The Robert Taylor Bailey Case

Killer Dies

Robert Taylor Bailey

Robert Taylor Bailey, a 20-year-old army deserter was arrested after a dust up with California State Highway Patrol in Santa Maria on September 7, 1942. Bailey, a native of Hattiesburg, Mississippi, deserted from Fort Benning, Georgia, on September 3, 1942. He was charged with the rape-slaying of two social workers in Wisconsin: Miss Neil John Pietrangeli and Miss Dorothy Baun. He was hitchhiking when the two young women picked him up, believing they were assisting a G.I. Although brutalized and shot with a stolen service revolver, Baun lived long enough to tell the tale and create a nationwide manhunt.

Bailey confessed, recanted and then implied he had a friend who aided him in the robbing, raping, and murders.

Ultimately, Bailey was sentenced to life in prison on the two first degree murder charges. For Baily, this term was about two years. In 1945, he died of a "mild brain infection" while in the prison hospital.

Downtown Santa Maria, September 7, 1942. Picture was taken by Ken Moore and was picked up by the AP and UP wire services and distributed across the United States.

Thomas Clayton Hilton Case

In what can only be termed a speedy resolution, Thomas Hilton, 30 died in the gas chamber February 1947, fourteen months after his arrest. The grandson of T. C. Nance, a prominent Santa Maria Valley pioneer, Hilton married in August of 1937. All was not well with the marriage and, in 1940, he became obsessed with murdering his wife, Mary.

Hilton was seemingly deferred from service in World War II because, although he was a truck driver, he was missing the index and middle finger on his right hand. He had been a sheet metal apprentice.

Mrs. Sue Fouts, a visitor to Santa Maria and possibly a casual, cocktail bar acquaintance, became the outlet for Hilton's marital frustrations. He "impulsively" murdered her with his pocket knife, slicing her from ear to ear, then chopped her brutally with an axe before dumping her naked body on highway 166 near Glines Summit, December 5, 1945.

Hilton, 6 foot 2 inches tall and weighing 170 pounds, was apprehended by officers on December 11, 1945, at approximately the same time as the body was being discovered by her nephew, Allan Stewart. She was face down in a gully, partially devoured by animals. A stolen truck was found abandoned and blood-spattered. He had transported and dumped the body and then ditched the truck in Bakersfield.

Hilton plead not guilty, then not guilty by reason of insanity and then not guilty again to murder in the first. He was additionally charged with stealing the truck, which was the property of Corbett Transportation Company.

Mrs. Sue Fouts had been in Santa Maria to assist her ailing mother and was also visiting her sister, Mrs. Nora Stewart, on East Stowell Road. She had been wearing a house dress and light coat when she went missing. Her purse was left at the residence the night she disappeared.

Hilton died when cyanide pellets were dropped into a chamber in which he was restrained. He played records the night before his execution and ate a hearty meal that morning. He is buried in the Santa Maria Cemetery.

Thomas Hilton Weds In Tonopah

Word has been received here of the marriage of Thomas Hilton, son of Mrs. Carrie Hilton of Santa Maria, to Miss Mary Leets of Lone Pine, in Tonopah. Nev., this morning.

Thomas Hilton, who has been employed in the mines in Trona, is a member of one of Santa Maria valley's pioneer families, and is a grandson of the late T. C. Nance. His bride is the daughter of Fred Leets, mining engineer in the Trona mines and Mrs. Leets, who is superintendent of Kern county public schools.

Missing Woman Believed Dead, Hilton Sought

Blood Stained Truck And Axe Clues In Fouts Case

The finding in Bakersfield of an abandoned truck, spattered with blood and containing a blood smeared axe, has led to the transmitting by the local police department of an all points bulletin to pick up Thomas Hilton, 28, of Santa Maria, on "suspicion of murder," according to Police Chief W. T. Feland.

James M. Noriega: Triple Homicide

The most difficult aspects of many murder cases are the denial and total lack of remorse expressed by the defendant. Somehow the murderer believes the victim got what they deserved or continues to deny guilt under the burden of irrefutable evidence. Such is the presentation of the case of James Manuel Noriega in the triple homicide of his 21-year-old girlfriend, her 2-year-old daughter and her unborn infant daughter.

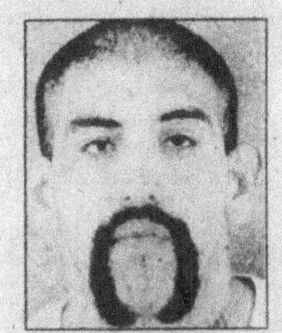
James Noriega

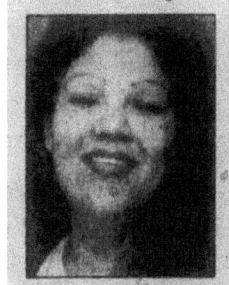 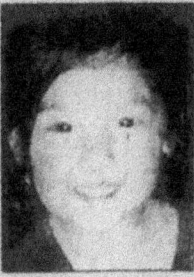
Kathleen Martinez   Savanna Zamora

For the families in this case, the pain was additionally exacerbated by delays. The murders of Kathleen Martinez, Savanna Starleen Zamora, and Maryann Rose Martinez were perpetrated July 16/17, 2001, but the trial and sentencing for Noriega was delayed until January 20, 2006.

James Manuel Noriega was identified as the victim's boyfriend. They were cohabitating at the Palms Motor Motel, room 11. The circumstances surrounding the triple homicide, the first in Santa Maria's history, are disturbing in the fact that so much was done to disguise the crime, the victims were very young and, other than a possible domestic dispute, there doesn't seem to have been a motive for the killings. Kathleen was strangled to death, Savanna was smothered, and the unborn child died of a lack of oxygen due to the mother's death. Noriega was arrested the day the bodies were discovered. The victim's bodies were found nude and covered in a soapy film in the bottom of the shower in the motel bathroom. The room itself was stripped clean, and the smell of bleach pervaded the small space.

> Tuesday jurors viewed a blue tank top, blue sweatpants and black jeans, each item discolored as if it had been stained with bleach.

The wheels of justice seemed to grind almost to a stop as far as Kathleen's family members were concerned. Both the defense and the prosecution protested that the delays were necessary to ensure the truth was told and justice was served. The big delay was the ongoing litigation of The People of The State of California vs. Benjamin Ballesteros. Filed November 2003, the challenge was focused on the diversity of the jury which would pass judgement on the defendant. The question was pertaining to whether or not the jury reflected, as is directed by the sixth amendment of the United States Constitution, a contingency of members that reflected the accused's ethnicity or fair cross-section of the community. Santa Barbara County was directed to change the two-step way jury members were recruited to serve at the courthouse. The decision was overturned by the Court of Appeals stating the current process was not biased.

> ▶ Ruling in June said system was race neutral

However, this case held up nearly 50 others including that of James Noriega.

Everything finally in place, the trial proceeded. Noriega was convicted June 2005. The prosecution wanted the death penalty. The family wanted him to sit in prison and suffer his choices and incarceration. The defense argued that this was an anomaly in his life "if" he was truly guilty. The prosecution pointed to a lack of remorse. Ultimately, the jury decided on life without the possibility of parole. Noriega arrived on 1/20/2006 at Mule Creek State Prison where he will spend the rest of his natural life.

The jury wasn't prepared to give the death penalty. The defense made a case for the future ability of DNA to provide exculpatory evidence. There was some DNA that didn't fit the picture drawn by the prosecution. Interesting since reasonable doubt should have compelled the acquittal of Noriega. It can only be inferred that there was no reasonable doubt in the minds of the jurors when it came to his guilt. A death sentence was more than they wanted to attach to Noriega. To date, he is still incarcerated and no new trial, details or evidence have been established.

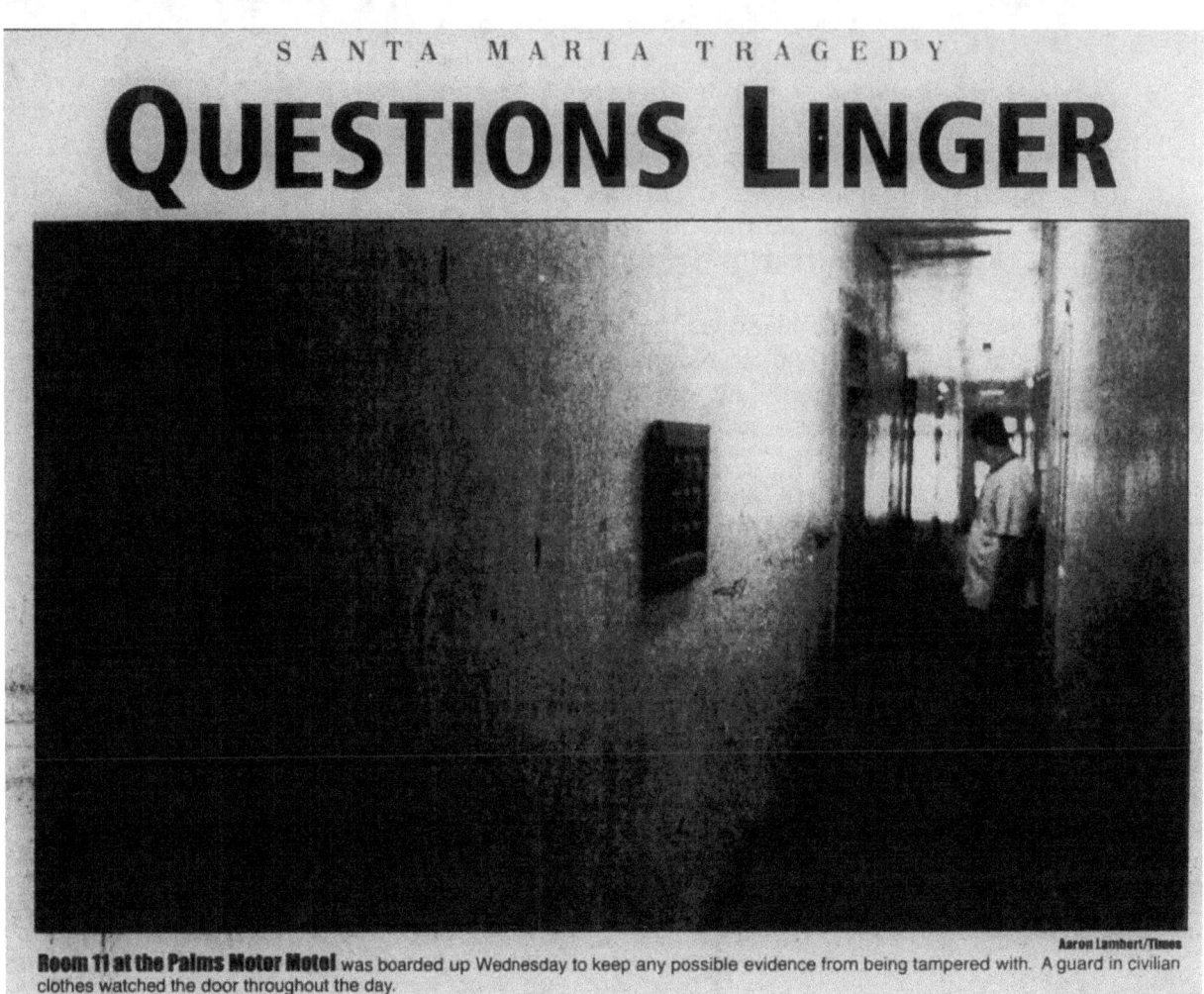

Room 11 at the Palms Motor Motel was boarded up Wednesday to keep any possible evidence from being tampered with. A guard in civilian clothes watched the door throughout the day.

Chapter 7: Missing-Exploited-Abused

The Missing and Unidentified Persons section in the California Department of Justice was created to assist law enforcement agencies and criminal justice organizations locate missing persons and identify unknown live and deceased persons. This is accomplished through a variety of techniques that are collectively called forensics. Examples include using the comparison of physical characteristics such scars, tattoos, or disfigurements from photographs or digital media. Fingerprints, DNA and dental/body X-rays are also tools used to identify people who cannot or will not self-identify.

In California, a missing person is someone whose location is unknown to the reporting individual. This includes any child who may have run away or have been taken involuntary. It also applies to a child taken illegally, detained or concealed by a noncustodial parent or nonparent family member.

Contrary to many beliefs, there is no waiting period required to report a person missing. All California police and sheriffs' departments must accept any report of a missing person, including runaways, and, without delay, give priority to the handling of the report.

Hobo

This man, said to have been a hobo for over 25 years working on mines, lumber camps and farms, was photographed in December 1938.
©Dorthea Lang/News Dog Media

June 27, 1938, Jack Dymond had been missing for three years. The story goes that he had been found in a pauper's grave in Santa Maria. Dymond was a Los Angeles County DA investigator. At the time of his disappearance, he was engaged in widely varied investigations, including digging into "underworld" vice, political protection and payoffs, and gambling operations. Everything about his assignment portended danger.

The pauper in the grave was a hobo, a tramp. He lived and existed among the excluded of society. In some ways this pose, one Dymond was greatly associated with, probably made Dymond invisible and seemingly unimportant as he moved around investigating all manner of criminal behavior. Dymond's disappearance in June 1935 sent a chill through the spines of all investigators.

Mrs. Mable Dymond, the wife, a resident of Pismo Beach found an obscure reference to a man found dead in a 'hobo jungle' in Guadalupe on June 10, 1938. The pauper had been tentatively identified as Jack Dymond. She contacted District Attorney Buron Fitts, who in turn reached out to the Santa Barbara Sheriff's Office. From a picture, the body was presumed to be Dymond.

It had been alleged that Dymond had been kidnapped and "taken for a ride" by underworld characters and given a "dirt nap." Mrs. Dymond had received the newspaper clipping with the claim this was her husband and where she could find him. The body was exhumed.

In a very convoluted explanation of events, new information came to light in the case of missing person Jack Dymond. There was a warrant for his arrest on a charge of criminal attack on a 15-year-old girl. Dymond disappeared on the day the warrant was issued. Dymond had been leading a clean-up campaign against Los Angeles city administrators. It had been charged that Dymond had relations with two young girls, statutory rape, ages 13 and 15. Dymond was dually fleeing prosecution, and a hit was placed on him by the unlawful characters he had been infiltrating and investigating. Everyone was out to get Jack Dymond on the day he disappeared. Is Dymond the pauper discovered in a box car, dead of a cerebral hemorrhage and buried in a grave in Santa Maria? The answer is "No." The body exhumed on June 29, 1938, is not Jack Dymond according to fingerprints. The mystery of Jack Dymond's disappearance remained unsolved a bit longer. His case remained open. He was a wanted man.

On September 6, 1940, Jack Dymond, one-time investigator for District Attorney Thomas L. Woolwine, was arrested in San Francisco on an outstanding warrant for rape. He was identified by fingerprints when he applied for a job as a guard of a wartime defense industry in San Francisco.

Jack Dymond, now 67 years old, slightly paunchy with a shiny bald head rimmed with sandy gray hair, faced the charges against him. He was told that Mary A. Flynn, 15, accused him of raping her on April 1, 1935, at his apartment on 512 West First Street. Dymond called it a frame-up. Flynn, now living in Oregon was loath, according to sources, to face and repeat her accusation in a Los Angeles courthouse. Finally, charges were dismissed as it was determined that the statute of limitations had expired. Dymond is a free man and the mystery is solved as well as resolved.

Kidnapping of Ben Stowell

It was a routine traffic stop until it became a kidnapping. Captain Ben Stowell got a message that a car with three youths had skipped Buellton without paying for their gas. He is in his police car, red light flaring and spotlight focused on the middle of the street at Boone and Broadway. The suspect car arrived at 7:45 p.m. and encountered Stowell. He ordered the trio out of the car. The driver was frisked and the second man, who was reposed in the back seat, was instructed to exit the vehicle. Neither of these men had a weapon, but the third man, seated passenger side, made his move; exiting the car he pushed a revolver into the side of the police chief and forced him into the back seat. Stowell would later describe the third man as the leader and a tough bird. Stowell made a desperate grab for the gun and was about to get the better of the assailant when the front seat passenger turned around and took Stowell's service revolver, a .38

G-Men Join in Stowell Kidnap Hunt in State

Search for the three youthful abductors of Police Capt. Ben Stowell continued throughout California today with Federal Bureau of Investigation agents joining the manhunt.

A representative of the Department of Justice was in Santa Maria to confer with police and sheriff's officers regarding the case.

No clues had been uncovered despite the state-wide search and no trace had been found of the abductors' car.

POLICE CAPTAIN KIDNAPED BY YOUTHFUL TRIO

Ben Stowell Made Prisoner As He Halts Car On South Broadway

Special Smith and Wesson. The scuffle was over; Stowell was a prisoner, and they were on the road to who knows where.

Within ten minutes police officers were on the trail of the abductors. The alarm spread by Leland Lutnesky, a witness to the kidnap and operator of the service station at Boone and Broadway, cried out on behalf of Stowell.

Captain Deane Laughlin

Captain Deane Laughlin and Night Officer H.H. Bittner called all law-enforcement agencies in the area to be on the lookout. The message was spread by teletype, radio and shortwave as police around the two counties sought to set-up blockades and thwart the escape to no avail. The car managed to elude capture by using dark alleys and back roads to skirt law enforcement. For seventy miles, Stowell was their prisoner, held at gun point with his own service revolver. Stowell talked to them about the escalation of their crime from petty larceny to felony kidnap. He stayed in their ear as they drove at breakneck speed around curves and corners. At one point, two of the men wanted to return Stowell. The "tough bird" denied that opportunity. Finally, a decision was made to let him go. An hour and 45 minutes after his capture, at 9:30 p.m., Stowell was released a short distance from the junction of the Maricopa highway and Ojai-Ventura road. They had intended to handcuff him to a signpost, but Stowell told them he didn't have any handcuffs on him; they were, however, secreted under his overcoat. To avoid being shot as they drove away, Stowell dropped to the ground quickly behind some heavy brush roadside. The car peeled away in a pall of smoke. Stowell was free, but the vehicle did manage to evade the roadblocks and escape into the dark fog of night.

Stowell tried flagging down a couple of cars, but no one came to his aid. After all, here was a man in an overcoat standing in the middle of the road waving his arms wildly for assistance with no visible form of transportation nearby to suggest how he got so far from town. Eventually a car did stop and took him to Maricopa and, from there, he was taken on to Taft where Santa Maria officers awaited him. He returned back to Santa Maria about 4 a.m. His abductors were in the wind, gone.

The first man, Charles Weston Ingold would be arrested in Denver on a federal warrant after trying to rob a post office and post boxes. The other two, Carl M. Grebb and William Arthur Stevens, escaped were apprehended in San Diego in March 1939. Despite the efforts of the criminals to hide their faces in the dark from Stowell, he did identify them all. By the time the Santa Maria police caught up to the trio, they were already in the pen, one at Fort Leavenworth and the other two at McNeil Island. The Santa Maria police department decided to hold charges until the end of their four-year prison sentences.

Now in Penitentiary

The three, who Capt. Stowell is confident are the three abductors, were identified as Charles Weston Ingold, Carl M. Grebb and William Arthur Stevens, all of Colorado. Ingold had been previously identified as one of the three abductors.

Ingold, Grebb and Stevens all are serving four-year terms in the federal penitentiary in Leavenworth following their recent conviction in Denver, on charges of robbing postoffice boxes. The Santa Maria police department will place "hold" orders on the men in an effort to prosecute them on the kidnaping charge after their federal sentence is completed. They are also wanted in Los Angeles on charges of looting postoffice boxes.

Unfortunately for Ben W. Stowell, justice would be delayed too long for him to savor it. He suffered a heart attack July 16, 1939, and died in the hospital. It was 217 days since his kidnapping. Stowell had calmly faced his abductors that night and told them, as they threatened his life, "we all gotta go sometime."

Lane Elwood Bryant

One of the greatest unknowns is why people do what they do. When one hears a familiar name attached to a crime, it is with shock and disappointment that the story unfolds. The Bryants are a pioneer valley family living in the community for more than one hundred years. When a member commits a bad act, it's shocking, a tragedy. It rocks not just the family, but the entire town.

In 1880 the business that became known as Bryant and Trott was owned and managed by Emmett Bryant. Three generations later, business was still booming. In 1980 Lane Bryant was the owner and manager of the well-known and beloved hardware store.

July 1985, 60-year-old Lane Bryant was charged with molesting a 5-year-old girl. Municipal Court Judge Barbara Beck ordered Bryant to stand trial in Superior Court on four counts of committing lewd and lascivious acts with a child. Bryant was also facing a special allegation of engaging in substantial sexual conduct with a child under 11 years of age and occupying a position of special trust. Bryant was arrested June 24, 1985, at the police station and released on $20,000 bail. Accusations stemmed from assaults January 1 through June 1, 1985. His preliminary hearing was scheduled for July 22, 1985.

November 1985, Bryant was sentenced to six years in state prison after pleading no contest to one count of the charges in a plea bargain. Instead of facing up to 14 years, he faced a maximum of 8 and received 6. March 1986, his lawyer S. Jon Gudmunds, tried to get him released as Bryant was facing death threats at the incarceration facility, Sierra Conservation Camp in Jamestown, where he was serving his sentence. The department of corrections feared his life was endangered due to his type of crime according to his attorney. All appeals for release due to harm were denied at the time.

Lane E. Bryant passed away on March 26, 2000, of natural causes at a local hospital. His obituary reminded all that he was a member of the Emmett Bryant pioneer family that settled in our valley in 1870s and that he had attended Santa Maria High School and graduated in 1942½. He joined the United States Army Air Corps during WWII and became a distinguished pilot.

Michael Jackson Acquitted

Santa Maria was simply host to an international case. The alleged crimes did not occur in our jurisdiction. However, it was Santa Maria where the self-proclaimed "King of Pop" came to get justice.

For the most part Santa Marians went about their daily lives without giving much notice to the Michael Jackson trial, which didn't become the spectacle that many thought, and feared, it would be.

"Outside of the courthouse complex and Cook Street and Miller Street, Santa Maria really — other than our restaurants and hotels are full — hasn't had a lot of impact to it," said Mayor Larry Lavagnino.

The out-of-town reporters covering the trial for news agencies worldwide have been trying to encapsulate the character of Santa Maria in sound bites and brief sentences, including phrases like: "Unfashionable part of the Central Coast," "sleepy town," and "best known for broccoli and strawberries."

Emotions surrounding Jackson were as varied and expansive as any case in history. All that emotion had to be contained within the walls of our courthouse by Judge Rodney Melville.

Rodney Scott Melville was the presiding judge in Santa Barbara County's superior court in which Michael Jackson's 2005 child molestation trial was conducted and in which Jackson was acquitted.

There can be no underestimation that People v. Jackson was the biggest undertaking of Melville's time on the bench. Hounded for years by press and innuendo, Jackson finally found himself under charges in 2005. He was accused by a 13-year-old boy of child molestation. The case went to court with Melville appointed the presiding judge. Before the start of the trial, Melville banned cameras from the courtroom, put a gag order on both sides and managed a three-day jury selection procedure that held the world spellbound during the spring of 2005. Eight women and four men were designated. These jurors would face four months and 140 witnesses. It was their sworn duty to decide if he was Peter Pan or a pedophile and, having determined that, to declare to the world their decision.

The jury would ultimately deliberate seven days starting on June 3, 2005. Every juror maintained an amount of anonymity. When ultimately they were quoted, it was generally as, "Juror #3 or #9." A surprise to all of those locked out of the proceedings was when one female juror remarked how they had expected better evidence, "something a little more convincing." As everyone waited outside for the show that was Jackson's arrivals and departures, it seemed inconceivable that expectations were not met inside the courtroom.

At the conclusion, the jury gave a note for the judge to read out in court. They felt "the weight of the world's eyes upon us all" and that they had "thoroughly and meticulously" studied all of the evidence.

The note concluded with a plea, "We would like the public to allow us to return to our lives as anonymously as we came."

Now it was the judge's moment to speak on behalf of the people. "Mr. Jackson, your bail is exonerated, and you are released," Judge Rodney S. Melville said after the string of not-guilty verdicts was read.

Michael Jackson was released back to his public, both adoring and abhorring. He was bigger than life for, although his brand was tarnished and his family criticized, he was a free man and innocent in the eyes of the law.

On June 25, 2009, four years after his trial, American pop singer Michael Jackson died of acute propofol and benzodiazepine intoxication at his home on North Carolwood Drive in the Holmby Hills neighborhood of Los Angeles. Paramedics treated Jackson at the scene, but he was pronounced dead at the Ronald Reagan UCLA Medical Center. His death would later be ruled a homicide, involuntary manslaughter.

Jackson's death triggered emotional responses around the world. Universally his work, his music, was revered, and his untimely death created a resurgence in purchases of his product. Internet searches and a spike in sales of his music nearly crippled a system built to answer world traffic. A televised memorial service was held on July 7, 2009, at the Staples Center in Los Angeles. It was viewed by an estimated 2.5 billion people globally. In 2010, Sony Music Entertainment signed a $250 million deal with Jackson's estate to retain distribution rights to his recordings until 2017 and to release seven posthumous albums over the decade following his death.

The "King of Pop," he is best remembered for his revolutionary videos such as "Thriller" and "Dangerous." Arguably, he was the most successful entertainer of all time with 13 Grammy Awards, 13 number one single hits in a solo career, sales of over 750 million albums worldwide and the greatest selling album of all time, "Thriller." His trademark single-sequined white glove and the Moonwalk were just part of his signature, his legacy. Born Michael Joseph Jackson in Gary, Indiana, the seventh of nine children, whether saint or sinner, he passed into the pages of history. He was flesh and blood, not immortal but gone at 50.

James Harrison Gamble

Satanic worship ring unveiled here

In May 1985, convicted child molester James H. Gamble, 60, of Santa Maria, was sentenced to one year in county jail. Superior Court Judge Royce Lewellen was swayed by some important character witnesses it would seem. Letters from Mayor George Hobbs, City Councilman Jack Adam, Henri Ardantz, Clarence Minetti and purportedly 35 other local residents wrote to the court on behalf of James H. Gamble, a masonry contractor.

40 local juveniles believed practicing sadism, masochism

Gamble was arrested on September 25, 1984, after a half-year investigation by the Santa Maria police department. A complaint of sadomasochistic acts and satanic worship involving about 40 area youths 14-17 years of age was revealed by the police. Some of the acts occurred at Gamble's home on the 500 block of South Oakley Avenue. Originally Gamble was arrested for possession of narcotics and possession of marijuana for sale. It was alleged his connection was mostly about providing drugs. In conversations with police, new allegations arose concerning Gamble.

Sexagenarian Gamble claimed he and his 15-year-old victim were having a love affair and considering marriage. Gamble plead guilty to two counts of unlawful sexual intercourse with a minor and one count of committing lewd and lascivious acts with a child. Gamble admitted to officers that he was sexually involved with the juvenile and had been having intercourse with her since she was 13 years old.

His sexual molestation conviction resulted in a court order to undergo psychiatric evaluation at the state prison in Chino. The diagnostic report called Gamble an "essentially prosocial individual" who "became involved in an inappropriate sexual liason." The report added that Gamble does "not present a substantial risk to the community."

The county Probation Department had originally recommended Gamble be sentenced to seven years and four months in state prison. The department changed its recommendation to one year in county jail, however, after the court received several psychiatric evaluations of Gamble and a report by the state Department of Corrections -- which recommended he be granted probation.

Child molester gets one-year jail term

Jim Gamble passed away February 3, 2010, at age 85. Born in 1924, he lived in, and was a resident of, Santa Maria all of his life.

Hans Jorgen Kardel

Justice delayed is justice denied. It would seem this had been the strategy of a recalcitrant Hans J. Kardel, a prominent Santa Maria businessman. First charged in January of 2016, he remained out on bail for two years with propitious delays to jury selection and witness availability. In the meantime, his victims spent their years in therapy and in anxiety of the day and time they would meet their accuser in court.

Kardel denies in testimony ever touching grandkids

Claims sexual contact initiated by granddaughter

Hans Jorgen Kardel, 84, was charged with several counts of sexual penetration with a child under the age of 10 and 14, aggravated sexual assault of a minor, lewd and lascivious acts with a child under 14, sexual penetration by a foreign object, and attempt to dissuade a witness. Add a special enhancement of committing the offences with more than one child. The incidences originated as early as 2005 and again in 2009, 2010, 2012, 2013 and 2015.

A criminal protective order was filed against Kardel. He pleaded not guilty in February of 2016.

Kardel testified on his own behalf blaming his victims. The girls were referred to as Jane Doe 1 and Jane Doe 2 to provide them with as little public exposure as possible under the circumstances but without denying them the chance to face Kardel in front of a jury for an opportunity for justice.

The jury obviously established there was no fault on the part of the young girls and found Kardel guilty of thirteen counts of lewd acts upon a child under the age of 10, two counts of sexual penetration by a foreign object, two counts of lewd and lascivious acts upon a child and one count of oral copulation/sexual penetration with a child. A nice topper was a charge of one count of dissuading a witness from reporting a crime. Kardel had threatened that bad things would befall all if this case went forward.

The abuse took place over the course of a decade. The girls are now 15 and 18 years old. The prosecution brought home the weight of Kardel's betrayal when it was pointed out that he had a position of trust and love which he used to his own means.

During the trial, a "pretext" phone call between Kardel and the mother of the girls revealed once again that he blamed the girls, and then Satan, for tempting him. At no point in the process did Kardel ever seem to take responsibility for his behavior. It was his opinion that the girls had control.

Judge John McGregor sentenced Kardel, now 85, to 14 years in state prison, followed by an indeterminate sentence of 15 years to life. Kardel must serve 85% before he is eligible for parole. That would be 25 years, making Kardel age 110 before there was even a possibility of parole; essentially, he received a life sentence.

The judge denied Kardel's request for bail pending an appeal because the conviction was one of a violent felony. The judge seemed compelled to add that Kardel lacked any remorse for his actions and thus also denied him probation rather than the prison term.

This case was an especially difficult one to present because the convicted tried not only to delay and deny justice but pushed off his offences onto his victims thus forcing them into long years of litigation and difficult testimony. He made his child victims defend themselves in open court.

As a church deacon, his behavior caused the girls to distrust God and dislike church reported their mother. The girls remarked on how much pain there had been for their family. The abuse led Jane Doe 2 to self-harm and contemplate suicide.

As exemplified by this case, sexual violence has psychological, emotional, and physical effects on survivors. These effects are not easy to deal with, but, with the right help and support, they can be managed. There are many organizations that have been created to help sexual assault survivors heal. It can be a long way from surviving to thriving. Seeing the perpetrator punished can go a long way toward starting the process.

> "I have nightmares about the abuse," Doe 2 continued. "He took away my relationships with my grandma, my brother, my uncle, aunt and my two cousins. I miss them every day and wonder how my little cousins are doing and how I wish I was there to watch them grow up."
>
> Doe 2 recalled how she had to testify in front of people she'd never met, explaining in detail what Kardel had done to them. "But, I'm not a victim anymore. I'm a survivor, and I finally have a voice."

Hans J. Kardel entered Mule Creek State Prison (MCSP) on October 5, 2018. Mule Creek is a California State Prison for men, exclusively. It opened in June 1987 and covers 866 acres located in Ione, California, southeast of Sacramento. It has sensitive needs yards referred to as SNY. SNY inmates are segregated from the general prison population for their own wellbeing and protection. The majority of the inmates are gang dropouts, informants, sex offenders, and former law enforcement officers.

Inmate Name	CDCR #	Age	Admission Date	Current Location
KARDEL, HANS JORGEN	BH4953	88	10/05/2018	Mule Creek State Prison

Chapter 8: Arson

JAIL SET ON FIRE AGAIN.

On Tuesday afternoon a fire alarm was turned in on account of a fire at the jail and when the firemen arrived it proved to be the same old story of a couple of bums burning the bedding and their clothing in order to prove themselves as much of a nuisance as possible. As might be expected the fire chief and his men were thoroughly disgusted and well they might be. This makes about the fifth time the jail has been deliberately set on fire in the past six months. It seems there ought to be a way of stopping this uncalled wanton destruction of city property.

We believe that the building can be lined with sheet iron and also that the windows could be double screened to make it impossible for anyone to pass matches inside.

The fire was started by two inmates who had been arrested on a battery charge. One of them named Kumph took off all his clothes and together with the bedding set it on fire. After extinguishing the blaze, it was necessary for the authorities to buy him new clothes. It seems that a prisoner under these circumstances should be liable for an additional sentence.

Santa Maria Times, 27 March 1915

There is a difference between a pyromaniac and an arsonist. Pyromania is a mental illness characterized by impulsivity; arson occurs when someone intentionally sets a fire with the understanding that others could be harmed and often for financial advantage. To confuse things further, pyromaniacs are sometimes arsonists, but arsonists aren't always pyromaniacs.

In general terms, arson is defined as the deliberate and malicious burning of property and has three main elements: element one is the burning of property itself, element two is that the burning is incendiary in origin, and element three is that the burning was started with the intent of destroying persons, property or both.

Statistics reveal that most serial arsonists are young white males; nearly 60 percent of arson fires are set by perpetrators before their 18th birthday, and 80 percent are set before the perpetrator is 29 years old. The worst arsonist in American history is considered to be Thomas A. Sweatt. He is a convicted serial arsonist credited with more than 350 fires over a nearly 30-year period. When Thomas Sweatt saw an attractive man, he would follow him home, but, instead of talking to the object of his affection, he would set fire to the man's house or car. He was eventually caught and given a life sentence.

Santa Maria Fire Department

The first fire department in Santa Maria was started in 1904. The Fire Chief was Arthur S. MacLaughlin. He was appointed by the board of city trustees at a salary of ten dollars a month. Helping him were several volunteer firemen: Henry Yelkin; Isaac Miller, Jr.; Lindsay McMillan; Al Bunce; Bill Miller; Frank Jessee and George Brown. Their tools were a hand-drawn hose cart, some lengths of hose, nozzles and a few axes. One of their first big fires was at the old Exchange Hotel. It was built in 1880 by Sam Blosser but owned by T. C. Nance at the time it burned to ashes in 1908. The flames started in Black's Candy Store, next door to the Exchange Hotel. The flames spread through that old dried wood so quickly that the fire fighters could save nothing but the little nearby tailor shop owned by Adam Bucewicz.

Japan Town Fire

It isn't always easy to determine arson. In March 1919, fire broke out in the back of Minami's Hotel located on the east side of Japan town. The fire was a calamity for all Japanese businesses as one after another burned to the ground. It was not clear that the fire was accidental and there were many in Santa Maria and Guadalupe who were not fans of the growing prospering commercial ventures that were shaping parts of the town. Insufficient fire measures and strong winds escalated the fire to a point where the blaze could not be contained. Destroyed by the fire were the Minami Hotel, Inouye Hotel, Niida Barber Shop, Wada Hotel, Osuga Store, Kusatake Restaurant, Kitagawa Store, Kitajima Hotel, Inouye Restaurant and many other small Japanese owned and run stores. Both Japanese and the men of the Santa Maria Fire Department tried to extinguish the all-consuming blaze that lit up the whole town that night.

> **FLAMES SWEEP BLOCK IN GUADALUPE; LOSS WILL TOTAL $75,000**
>
> A fire, said to have started in a Chinese Joss house, swept a block and a half of Guadalupe's Main street early last evening, totally destroying 14 frame buildings, rendering approximately 200 people homeless and resulting in a financial loss of well over $75,000.

A major fire occurred January 18, 1924, at 7 p.m. Fire broke out at the Chinese Buddhist Temple and spread over to the Japanese business district. The damage was estimated altogether at well over $75,000 dollars. Businesses in this blaze were: Yamada Store, Nakae Store, Inouye-Ochi Store, Taniguchi Barber Shop, Furuya Hotel, Den Sugimoto, Bungo Matsubara, and Risaburo Awa.

> This is the fourth time that fire has destroyed different portions of Chinatown and the second time that this same side has been completely destroyed. That fire occurred about 16 years ago and the buildings destroyed Friday evening have all been built since that time.
>
> * * * *

Determining arson is so difficult because just by the nature of fire, evidence is destroyed. Sometimes arson is determined on the grounds of motive: insurance fraud or covering other crimes like robbery or murder. Chemical residuals, burn patterns and many new forensic techniques aid investigators today.

Thanksgiving Weekend Fire

The El Camino School fire on November 23, 1962, was considered the worst blaze in Santa Maria history. Fire Chief Harry Bell believed the blazing inferno was set with intension. It is considered that the fire was underway under the floor of the school for two hours before the alarm was sounded at 9:15 p.m. Evidence suggested that the fire probably started in two separate places under room 4, an eighth-grade classroom. Wiring and other probable natural causes were ruled out by investigators. Arson was a strong probability.

The 31-year-old school suffered over $300,000 in damage. Four classrooms, a janitor's room, a lavatory and the main hallway in the center wing were demolished by the inferno. Included in the loss were hundreds of desks, volumes of school books, classroom papers, and records as well as some student and faculty personal property. School did not resume at El Camino for some time (five days later the campus re-opened but not the main building), as clean-up was extensive. Because the state had a requirement of a mandatory number of school days and the school board wanted to avoid extending the school year for students, provisions were made to get kids into makeshift classrooms.

No one was ever prosecuted for the fire.

Bradley Hotel Fire

Arson Suspicion Mounts In Hotel Fire

The case for arson at the Bradley Hotel is convincing. Many believe there was foul play involved in the loss. There is evidence of multiple ignition points. Witness testimony given to fire investigators indicate they saw different points of origin that eventually joined together to create the incredible conflagration. The building was due for demolition. No gas or electric utilities were connected, and it was completely vacant at the time the fire ensued. The current hotel owner was John Ruffoni. Once the showplace of downtown Santa Maria, the hotel was originally built in the 1880s by Rueben Hart. It was a luxury destination with great amenities for travelers. Charles Bradley bought the hotel, which sits on the corner of Main Street and Broadway, and transformed it into a more modern facility during his time as owner, continuing its claim to elegance and comfort. The years were unkind to this once palatial

Arsonist on Spree
April 1963

Fire Dept. Checks 'Deliberate' Fires

Four separate fires, all deliberately set between 11:25 p.m. and 11:37 p.m. Wednesday caused extensive damage to four cars and also damaged other property, Fire Chief Harry Bell reported.

Firemen received the first call at 11:25 p.m. from Joaquin's Cocktail Lounge, 518 W. Main St., after fires were found in the front seats of two cars parked in the lounge parking lot.

The fires, in cars owned by Leo Vigil, 1839 N. Lincoln St. and Santos Talaugon, 1252 E Creston St. had no sooner been extinguished when a second call sent firemen racing to Holser and Bailey.

When firemen arrived in the company's warehouse area at 116 S. Pine St. they found that someone had piled and ignited trash on top of a gas meter. Heat from the fire caused the meter to rupture and firemen were forced to turn off the gas.

The third call, at 11:43 sent firemen to the rear of the Pastime Pool Room, 112 W. Main St., where they found a 1962 Ford owned by Duke Wilson, 516 W. Mill St. burning. Excelsior had been piled in the front seat and then touched off firemen said. The entire inside of the car was gutted before firemen could extinguish the blaze.

The final call was received at 11:37 from 127 W. Church where a 1951 Cadillac, owned by R.L. Walmsley was found burning. Firemen quickly extinguished the blaze and no extensive damage was reported.

Police, who also followed up the calls have taken one man into custody for questioning. He was booked on a loitering charge after police found him in the vicinity of the Holser and Bailey warehouse shortly after the trash fire there.

edifice that anchored downtown Santa Maria. Her glory days were long past, but why she was rushed off in a blaze of fire was suspicious to many.

Certain Of Arson

Fire officials seemed to have determined that the fire is the work of arson, and a charge of murder awaits the perpetrator or perpetrators. At 10:27 p.m. on April 27, 1970, two days before the fire took place, the building had been sealed after ridding it of vagrants who had taken up residence and often built fires in the old commodes. Further concerning investigator, there would have been no ground-level access for entry to a trespasser who might have scaled to an upper floor with the means to bring the building down in flames.

Highly tragic was the loss of a fireman. Alvin Newton was consumed by the fire when a wall buckled inward pulling him into the blaze as the roof collapsed. William Alvin Newton, 35, had been a volunteer firefighter and with the force for seven years. He was full time employed at the City of Santa Maria Water Department. He had attended local schools and worked for the city the past 15 years. He came to Santa Maria with his family from Oklahoma in 1946. Survivors include his wife Marilyn and three children. While there is much angst about the death of Firefighter Newton, there is also no hard evidence of whom to blame. To date, no one was ever charged with arson or the murder of Firefighter Newton.

Fire Truck Carries Alvin Newton's Body To His Grave

House Fires

Arson fire burns three homes

On May 21, 1976, at approximately 10:30 p.m., a farm labor dispute was named as the motive for an arson fire that caused $25,000 in damages to three farm worker's houses on the Jim Adam dairy, 1601 W. Main Street. One property was totally engulfed while a portion of the second property and most of the third were saved by fire fighters.

The fire was attributed to three disgruntled workers who were recently fired from the dairy, which has been the scene of recent labor conflicts. The fire was definitely arson with blazes starting in several

Farm worker's house on Adam Dairy shows effects of fire blamed on arson

places in all three structures and residue evidence of a flammable liquid present. Two other employees discovered the fires and alerted the foreman. Owner Chuck Adam called the county fire department.

January 1979, rewards of up to $500 were being offered through the confidential We Tip system for information leading to arrests and convictions on three recent arson fires in the Orcutt area. All three were private homes. For the first time in 50 years, the Federal Bureau of Investigation (FBI), has added arson to its original list of seven crimes.

Rewards offered for arson info

Arson investigators dig through ruins of Carmen Lane building
Digging for clues, from left, are Mike Butler, Jack Owen and Bill Rye

Fire gutted building value reduced by half

15 July 1980, Gasoline was the accelerant.

There are spite fires, cover-up fires, vanity fires and the "pyro" fires. Even with advanced fire investigation techniques, most arson fires never make it to the courtroom. There is so much reasonable doubt to be cast and created by savvy defenders. Fire by its very nature is unpredictable and thus misleading. A witness, a confession, obvious use of an accelerant or a clear economic motive can help investigators resolve some arson fires, but most go unsolved.

Economic Tough Times Spur increase in Arson

After economic hard times such as in 1982 and 1983, the frequency of arson incidents increases as many people "torch" homes or cars they no longer can afford.

That's the assessment of George Lopez, arson investigator for the Santa Barbara County Fire Department.

"Right now, in my opinion, we seem to be having a bigger problem (with arson)," Lopez said. "It seems like we're beginning to get more of them."

Lopez reports that at least 14 of 324 structure fires in the county last year were deliberately set. Arson was also determined as the cause of 27 grass or brush fires, five vehicle fires and four refuse fires.

Although he has not come across any known professional arsonists in the county, Lopez said he "wouldn't be surprised"

On July 22, 1991, politics seem to have sparked a 1:25 a.m. fire at Planned Parenthood on 415 E. Chapel. The fire was purposefully set on the outside by an accelerant ignited with an open flame devise investigators on scene reported. Damage was estimated at $10,000. Likely the perpetrators were messaging their concerns over the clinic's operation and trying to prevent services from being provided. Cheryl Rollings, executive director of Tri-Counties Planned Parenthood agency, promised quick restoration and hoped for arrests and prosecution of the arsonist(s). Fingers are pointed but no suspects loom.

Pro-life group condemns arson attack

Bruce Horner

Horner

Bruce Horner is an arsonist; the defense wanted to establish that he was a lower level of arsonist than prosecutors portray. No one disputes that Horner deliberately started fires that destroyed ten homes under construction in Santa Maria during the summer of 2003. Citing boredom and jealousy, the indigent Horner lacked any remorse. But as a jury trial commenced in March 2005, public defender Kurt Hamblet suggested that they weren't homes by definition under the law. Horner had previous arson convictions from March 2000, so the more serious "aggravated" charges prevailed. Despite the prolonged legal challenges, Horner received 40 years to life. At age 48 in September 2005, he should not be eligible for parole until 2045, making him 88. He was also fined $1.4 million dollars. However, a records search reveals that Horner is not incarcerated in 2021; he may have been a beneficiary of Governor Gavin Newsom's 76K early prison release plan.

Robert Scott Forsythe

He was a wildfire arsonist. He was also an Orcutt volunteer fireman. He was arrested and charged with arson by Sheriff's detectives. Sheriff John Carpenter and County Fire Chief W.J. Patterson announced the charges in August 1979. Forsythe's arrest was the culmination of a two-month investigation into series of grass fires in northern Santa Barbara County and southern San Luis Obispo County. Forsythe came under suspicion early during the investigation and investigators surveilled him. According to Detective Bruce Correll, friends and associates of Forsythe made important contributions to the investigation. Forsythe was implicated in a number of arson-started fires. It was hard to estimate the number of fires Forsythe was responsible for; "a good number," reported Correll.

Forsythe, 19, was released to his parents on his own recognizance. Deputy DA Mike Scott recommended the release. As part of the agreement, Forsythe, who smokes, has been ordered to do so only inside and in the presence of an older adult. He may not light his own cigarette.

Orcutt man scheduled for trial

Robert Scott Forsythe has been scheduled for jury trial on Sept. 15 in San Luis Obispo County Superior Court on two counts of wildland arson. Forsythe has been charged by the California Department of Forestry (CDF) on the two arson counts which occurred in the Nipomo area during July 1979. The 20-year-old resident of Orcutt, is waiting to serve a 180 day sentence in that county's jail after pleading guilty to three counts of solicitation to commit wildland arson in Santa Barbara County. The jail sentence will be followed by three years probation.

More Trouble for Forsythe

August 1983

Robert Scott Forsythe, 23, of Santa Maria was booked on a battery charge and a second suspect is being sought after Steven L. Viltrakis, 25, of Lompoc and Steven A. Smith, 31, of Grover City were assaulted outside Alexander's Harvest in the 1500 block of North Broadway today at 4:15 a.m., police report.

October 2002

Man accused of DUI after hitting post

A man was arrested Saturday evening on suspicion of drunken driving after he struck a railroad crossing post on the 600 block of South Depot.

Robert Forsythe, 42, of Santa Maria was transported to Marian Medical Center after the crash. He complained of chest pains.

Police said Forsythe had to be restrained by emergency personnel in order to be transported.

September 1990

A Santa Maria juvenile was arrested Friday in connection with a recent robbery, according to police.

The 17-year-old youth was arrested at 6:30 p.m. Friday in connection with a robbery that morning in the 200 block of west Orange Street.

Victim Robert Forsythe had his red 1977 Toyota pickup stolen at 12:16 a.m. and had his nose broken, his front teeth knocked out and his cheek broken by what he described as "several youths."

Town Center Inn Fire October 12, 2013

A suspicious fire dislocated 40-100 people. An early Saturday morning fire sent Santa Maria firefighters up ladders to rescue trapped residents at the old hotel located at 215 N. Broadway. Nearly 166 people lived at the 1930s era building. The fire burned fast and furious for about 45 minutes. The location was treated as a crime scene as the fire was of a suspicious nature.

OFFICIALS INVESTIGATING SUSPICIOUS DOWNTOWN BLAZE

Hotel fire sends 7 to hospital

It is believed the fire started in a front entryway. Residents reported hearing a pair of loud explosions.

December 2013, Amos Lee Andrews, 57, was charged with attempted murder, felony arson and residential burglary in the attack at the Town Center Inn. Prosecutors allege that Andrews used a Molotov cocktail to set off the blaze that broke out around 2:30 a.m. and gutted the inn.

Andrews was sentenced to 17 years in state prison. Age 57, appearing frail and wheeled into court in a wheelchair, Andrews made a plea agreement. He will have served 85% of his time before being eligible for parole in February 2026. He received 9 years for the attempted murder charge, 1 year 8 months for the arson, 1 year 4 months for burglary and 5 years for use of an accelerant in the arson.

Judge Rogelio Flores' courtroom was filled with victims of the fire who spoke out toward Andrews with great condemnation, indignation and frustration.

California Medical Facility (CMF) facilities include Level I housing, open dormitories without a secure perimeter. It is also known as "the California prison system's health care flagship."

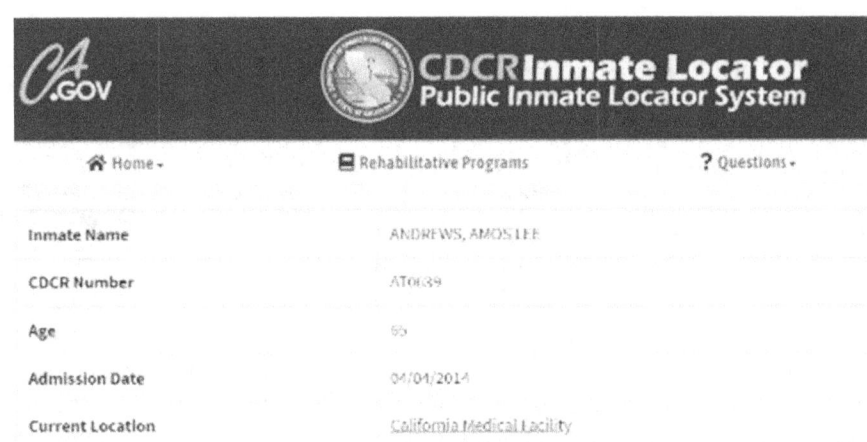

An accelerant-sniffing dog named Riley checks out the site Saturday for any sign of arson.

Inmate Name	ANDREWS, AMOS LEE
CDCR Number	AT0139
Age	65
Admission Date	04/04/2014
Current Location	California Medical Facility

Chapter 9: Evolution of Law Enforcement

It can be very frustrating to hear about crimes and then see the punishment that is meted out for the offences. Most of us have a strong sense of justice. The perception of fairness, where the punishment fits the crime, comes from a different place for all of us. Victim or perpetrator, there will be a sense of whether the outcome is right or wrong. It is the frustration that many have felt with the legal system that has resulted in more stringent guidelines for all involved in the judicial system. More rules for police, more rights for the accused and mandatory sentences by judges.

Basically the system needs to be held to a standard that permits everyone an equal opportunity under the law. It is at this point that both sides scream "Foul!". The burden of law enforcement has evolved greatly over our short American history. It has always been said that a person is deemed innocent until proven guilty, but plenty will dispute that statement. Ask anyone who has been fingerprinted and booked if they felt treated innocent. Of course, police do not arrest anyone they believe is not guilty. So where are we in the process? Bring on the attorneys! Only used car salesmen are held in less esteem than lawyers.

First Justice in Our Valley, January 1846

History in our valley virtually begins with William Benjamin Foxen. None disputed Foxen's reputation as an honest man. After he led Fremont to victory using an old Indian trail that had for some time been used as a short cut to Santa Barbara, over the San Marcos Pass in the Santa Ynez Mountains, he kindled the ire of those opposed to the Americanization of California. He had drawn a diagram and lead the way with his son William for Fremont's army. Down the length of Foxen Canyon, Foxen led Fremont's army, through the Zaca Rancho, over the steep Zaca ridge, through the site of the present town of Los Olivos and El Rancho Alamo Pintado to the banks of Alamo Creek, where the armed force made camp for the night. They preceded on the next day to Rancho San Marcos. Pouring rain and treacherous trails made the trek longer and more dangerous. Foxen returned home and left his son to finish the march into Santa Barbara. When Fremont entered Santa Barbara, it was all but deserted with forces deployed to Gaviota Pass waiting for him while the few remaining attended mass at the mission. Fremont quickly raised the American flag and declared victory; thus was Santa Barbara captured without bloodshed. And thus too did Foxen enrage the still powerful judicial system administered by those who opposed the Americanization of California.

The Californios were enraged with Foxen. They bribed bands of wild Indians to raid his rancho. Foxen was under constant siege after his return home. For the greater part of a year, Foxen battled to protect his rancho from constant destruction. Finally, fearing the danger was too great for his family, he determined to move them to the mission until he could secure Tinaquaic. Positioning his household in safe quarters, Foxen returned to pack up the rest of his possessions. On arrival he found his home ransacked but not empty. A man called Augustine bent on vengeance had cleared the adobe of all useful stuffs, including stock and dry goods. He was preparing to burn everything he couldn't carry away.

Foxen was unarmed but enraged. There was an ancient *carabine* that stood in the corner of the room. It had been out of commission and unused for a long time, but Foxen took it into his hands and declared, "Jesus Christ, if it is just that I defend my rights, let this weapon fire!" He stepped to the door and fired the gun. Augustine was struck and killed by the bullet. Foxen fled for his life. He made it on foot to the mission and was taken under authority. American courts were not yet established. *Alcaldes,* who had been elected or appointed, still administered the law. Pedro Carrillo, considered a ferocious man with a cruel nature and known for unjust decisions, was the Judge at Santa Barbara. Carrillo believed Foxen a traitor. Without a trial, Carrillo drew a knife to Foxen's throat as he was held from both sides by men stronger than himself. Foxen cried out, "For the love of Christ!" As he did so his shirt drew open in his struggle and on his exposed chest displayed to view was a large tattooed picture of the Christ with the crown of thorns on His brow.

His executioner fell back. Carrillo would not cut his throat. He incarcerated Foxen instead. Governor R.B. Mason sent a letter of instruction to Judge Pedro Carrillo. He was ordered to hold a special court for the trial of Foxen, appointing Estavan Ardisson as an additional judge. The jury was to consist of six Americans and six Californios.

How the trial actually played out is lost to historians, but Bancroft's *History of California* relates that Benjamin Foxen killed a man for stealing his chickens and was found guilty of manslaughter and sentenced to four years' imprisonment. Foxen never served a day but was given immediate freedom. Thus justice was first preserved.

Miranda

If you've ever watched a single cop show, you've heard of "Miranda." What does it mean to law enforcement or to an arrested person? Most of us know there is a recitation given the person being taken in by the police. "Read him his rights!" So how did our rights get dwindled down into one simple word, Miranda?

"A Miranda warning" refers to the requirement that once an individual is detained by the police, there are certain warnings a police officer is required to give to a detainee. These warnings stem from the Fifth Amendment privilege against self-incrimination and the Sixth Amendment right to counsel.

MIRANDA WARNING
1. YOU HAVE THE RIGHT TO REMAIN SILENT.
2. ANYTHING YOU SAY CAN AND WILL BE USED AGAINST YOU IN A COURT OF LAW.
3. YOU HAVE THE RIGHT TO TALK TO A LAWYER AND HAVE HIM PRESENT WITH YOU WHILE YOU ARE BEING QUESTIONED.
4. IF YOU CANNOT AFFORD TO HIRE A LAWYER, ONE WILL BE APPOINTED TO REPRESENT YOU BEFORE ANY QUESTIONING IF YOU WISH.
5. YOU CAN DECIDE AT ANY TIME TO EXERCISE THESE RIGHTS AND NOT ANSWER ANY QUESTIONS OR MAKE ANY STATEMENTS.

WAIVER
DO YOU UNDERSTAND EACH OF THESE RIGHTS I HAVE EXPLAINED TO YOU? HAVING THESE RIGHTS IN MIND, DO YOU WISH TO TALK TO US NOW?

So why do we need Miranda if we have the Fifth and Sixth Amendments? The answer is simple: because most do not know their rights under the constitution. In *Miranda v. Arizona*, 384 US 436 (1966), the Supreme Court validated these rights and thus was created the term. Without a Miranda warning or a valid waiver of the Miranda rights, statements made may be inadmissible at https://www.law.cornell.edu/wex/trial under the exclusionary rule, which prevents a party from using https://www.law.cornell.edu/wex/evidence at trial what had been gathered in violation of the United States Constitution.

Ernesto Arturo Miranda mug shot.

Ernesto Miranda was arrested at his home on March 13, 1963, and taken into custody to a police station where he was not positively identified in a line-up as her attacker by the victim. He was then interrogated without being informed of his right to remain silent or to have an attorney present. After two hours of questioning, Miranda confessed to the kidnapping and rape of the eighteen-year-old concession stand worker at the Phoenix movie theatre. His trial began on June 20, 1963. Miranda's confession and four witnesses made up the entire prosecution's case. He was found guilty June 27th and sentenced to 20-30 years imprisonment on each count. An appeal was filed claiming Miranda's constitutional rights were abridged. The Arizona Supreme Court disagreed and upheld the conviction. Without an attorney, Miranda appealed to the United States Supreme Court, where two lawyers took up his argument *pro bono*. The Supreme Court of the United States decided on June 13, 1966, in a five-to-four decision, that his rights had been violated. Later without the confession presented in evidence, Miranda was retried and found guilty and thus his sentence was upheld in the end. This landmark case led to all arrested persons being read their rights as they exist under the Fifth and Sixth Amendments. Miranda was made famous.

Loopholes:

1. Police conduct an interrogation but the suspect is **not** taken into custody. For example, detectives leave their business cards at the home of a person involved in the investigation. If that person who received the card contacts the detective of their own volition, agrees to come to the police station to answer some questions, and the detective does not detain or arrest the person during the questioning, there is interrogation but no custody, so the detective is not obligated to read the Miranda Rights.

2. The suspect is in custody but the police **don't** conduct an interrogation. For example, two subjects are arrested at the same time and placed in the back of a patrol car. Unknown to the two subjects, police have a recording device on in the vehicle so they can record what the subjects are talking about. One or both suspects may make incriminating statements. The two subjects are in custody but, because no police officer is asking the questions, there is no interrogation so the police officer is not obligated to read the Miranda Rights to them.

3. A "pretext" phone call is another example. The call is usually between the victim and the perpetrator with law enforcement recording and listening to the call. The one being

investigated is led to incriminate himself in conversation with the victim or a coconspirator. There is no obligation to read the Miranda Rights as law enforcement has neither custody nor is interrogating.

Ernesto A. Miranda, The Man

Miranda served eleven years of his sentence before being granted parole. His famous appeal helped earn him notoriety and money after his release. He autographed Miranda Warning cards for a price. Unfortunately, Miranda was not reformed by his contribution to the legal system or his time in prison. Numerous arrests followed for driving offenses which eventually led to a suspension of driving privileges. Once found in the possession of a fire arm, in violation of his parole conditions, he was returned to prison for another year. After his rerelease, Miranda spent his time hanging out in bars and living in cheap motels. In 1976, while playing cards at the La Amapola Bar in Phoenix, a violent confrontation transpired. Ernesto A. Miranda was mortally wounded with a knife and pronounced dead on arrival at the Good Samaritan Hospital at the age of 34. A suspect was arrested and read his Miranda rights. While awaiting trial, he fled to Mexico. No extradition was made, and the case was subsequently closed.

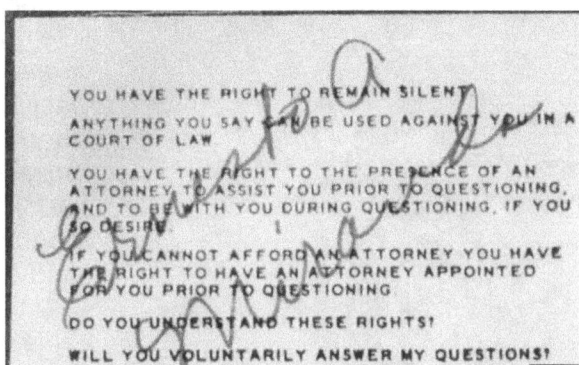

Autograph copy of a Miranda Warning Card

POST: Commission on Peace Officer Standards and Training

The Commission on Peace Officer Standards and Training (POST) was established by the Legislature in 1959 to set minimum selection and training standards for California law enforcement. The California POST is the PELLETB. PELLETB stands for POST Entry Level Law Enforcement Test Battery and is an entry-level written exam recommended by the Commission. The PELLETB is two-and-one-half hours long and covers five or six sections.

The old days of someone knowing someone and thus getting a uniform, badge and gun have gone the way of other good ol' boy traditions. Entrusting our communities' legal health and safety to good intentioned, untrained, but well liked, individuals has been countered by some hefty requirements.

The five (six sections) in this 1 hour, 15 minute-test:
1. **Writing** - Clarity
    Multiple-choice - choose sentence most clearly written
2. **Writing** - Spelling
3. ***CLOZE** Reading Test

---

*A **CLOZE Reading Test** presents a written passage with words omitted. The number of characters for each missing word is shown in place of the word as a series of dashes. The applicant must fill in the correct word using his or her knowledge of context, good grammar, spelling and vocabulary. CLOZE is considered difficult by most applicants because: (1) they have never seen this type of test before and (2) there are no answer choices given.

Fill in the missing words in a passage
4. **Reading Comprehension - 25 questions in 25 minutes**
    Read a policy or procedure and answer questions about it based only upon the information presented

5. **Writing – Vocabulary**
6. ***Logical Reasoning**
    Multiple-choice - Information grouping, ordering, classification and relationships

Basic Training Academies are located all around the state. Allen Hancock College offers a certificate in policing at its Lompoc Valley campus. The Public Safety Training Complex is one of Allan Hancock College's most prestigious Measure I-funded projects. The $38 million facility houses the college's police, fire, emergency medical services, and environmental technology programs. The state-of-the-art complex includes a six-story fire tower, one-mile Emergency Vehicle Operations course, a 'scenario' village, shooting range, fitness track and obstacle course.

This is a basic overview of requirements for peace officer training, the minimum and the tip of the iceberg for becoming a police officer. On-going training, new technology and advancing forensics ensures that anyone who decides to become an active part of law enforcement will be adequately prepared, educated and psychologically suited to wear the uniform, badge and gun.

Private Investigators and Security

The practice and profession of private investigation began with Allan Pinkerton. Pinkerton was a cooper (one that makes or repairs wooden barrels and tubs), abolitionist, detective, and spy. He established the Pinkerton National Detective Agency in 1850. Pinkerton became famous when he thwarted a plot to assassinate then President-elect Abraham Lincoln in 1861. Pinkerton agents performed services from undercover inquiries and detection of crimes to factory defense and armed security. At its pinnacle of existence, the number of Pinkerton National Detective Agency active agents and reserves rivaled the number of active soldiers and reserves in the United States Army. In 1856, Allan Pinkerton hired Kate Warne as a private detective, making her the first female private detective in the United States. Pinkerton agents were hired to hunt down outlaws the likes of Jesse James, the Reno brothers, and Butch Cassidy and the Sundance Kid.

Many private investigators with special academic and practical experience often work with defense attorneys on capital punishment and other criminal defense cases. Some are insurance fraud investigators. There are also what are referred to as merchant patrolmen, which is any person employed by a merchant's patrol agency to guard or protect persons or property, money, securities or other valuables, or patrol streets, districts, or territory for such purposes.

---

*Reasoning may or may not appear on your specific exam. California POST says that it will be standard for all agencies in the near future.

Benjamin Fredrick James

BENJAMIN F. JAMES

Benny James was a lifelong criminal who finally met his match in a merchant patrolman. In the early morning of December 5, 1950, a merchant patrolman in Santa Maria observed a man crouching on the porch of Santa Maria High School. Bruno "Joe" Zemaitis was finishing his nightly tour of duty. Zemaitis ordered the skulking figure to come out and identify himself. As the shadow left the porch, Zemaitis saw him toss something into shrubbery that had partially obscured him in the beginning. Zemaitis decided to handcuff the man and then ask his questions. One cuff in place, Benny James pulled away, struck the merchant patrolman and took off running. Zemaitis called a warning to stop and then fired several shots at the suspect. The last shot took effect dropping James to the ground dead. The burglary career of Benjamin Frederick James, alias Rodney E. Blackey, has abruptly ended.

Zemaitis after the shooting of Benny James on December 5, 1950

If James would have had a media name, it would likely have been the "High School Burglar." The basic investigative technique of *modus operandi* nailed Benny James. Communication between authorities put him on the map. Zemaitis put him in the dirt.

James' first arrest for a schoolhouse burglary was in 1933. He was sentenced to six months in county jail for this offense. Next he was arrested in Los Angeles in 1935; this time he was granted ten years probation on the condition he serve 90 days in county jail. James was next arrested in 1938 where he was charged with the burglary of Fortuna High School in Eureka. He was sentenced to San Quentin but paroled early in 1940. He was arrested two days later on a parole violation and returned to prison for a period until 1941. On May 7, 1945, James burgled a combined high and grammar school in Chowchilla, California. November 25, Amador Valley Joint Union High School suffered a burglary and another at Pleasanton. On the 28th, the same *modus operandi* occurred at Sebastopol High School. The crime was repeated using the same methods, taking the same treasures. It was presumed to be the same perpetrator, and there were even more crimes with this signature. Various police agencies rallied around the technique or M.O. and put the word out via assorted law enforcement publications: be on the look-out for a high school bandit.

Three more schools were hit in early December. Zemaitis knew to be on guard at the high school. Zemaitis dropped James on December 5, 1950. He immediately reported the shooting to law enforcement. It was quickly discovered that James had broken into the high school through a window and, using his same M.O., had burgled Santa Maria High School of a sizable amount of cash. What he had tossed surreptitiously into the shrubs that night were his burglary tools: drills, screw drivers, jack hammer and flashlights. Eventually evidence led law enforcement on a trail of his robberies. His car was located and then his apartment. Each new discovery led to more and more loot! Plenty of money was discovered. He'd been careful to hit schools when they had the most of cash on hand.

He hadn't bargained for a merchant patrolman.

Keith Bennett

On December 10, 1957, burglary suspect Keith Bennett was shot and wounded by merchant patrolman Bruno J. Zemaitis. The 22-year-old Camp Cooke soldier was thieving inside of Tom's Market on South Broadway.

Zemaitis had found the back door of the market forced open at 12:45 a.m. Entering the establishment, Zemaitis called out to Tom Simlar, the store owner. A man stepped toward Zemaitis with a tire iron in hand. Zemaitis warned him to get to the ground. According to Zemaitis, the suspect continued menacingly toward him. Zemaitis warned him again and then shot the man 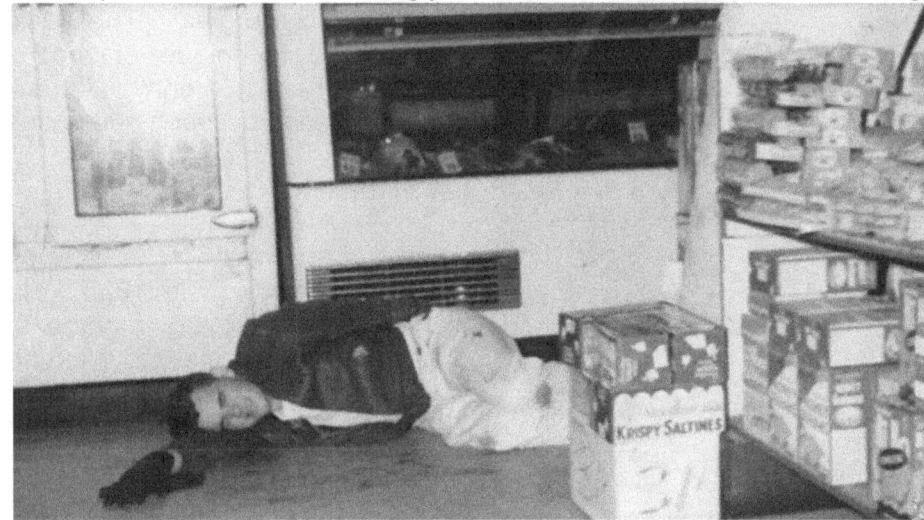 close range, once in the wrist and then the abdomen. Bennett was a cook at the Army disciplinary barracks. A paper bag with several dollars ($12.62) in change was found on him. It was surmised by sheriff's officers that he also attempted a brake-in across the street at Del Monte Market. Bennett survived his wounds.

Defund the Police

"Defund the police" is a slogan that refers to divesting public money from police departments. The term suggests that money is wasted on the police and that reallocating funds to non-policing forms of public safety and community support, such as social services, youth services, housing, education, healthcare and other community resources would be a more productive process for serving the people.

Another opinion is that this could lead to vigilantism and private police forces and that only a select few would have protection under the law.

Santa Maria Chiefs of Police

Constables 1885-1904   Matt Jessee
                                Alex Samson
                                John Waugh
                                I.W. "Doc" Southard

Chiefs
1905-1912	Garrett L. Blosser
1912-1916	Henry H. Bardin
1916 (Five months Aug-Dec)	Hubert M. Cole
1917 (Less than one month Jan)	Henry Kortner
1917 (Six months Jan-July)	Alfred F. Black
1917-1919	Jesse B. Armstrong
1919 (One month-April)	T.S. Lofthouse
1919-1921	A.C. (John) Ramsey
1921-1926	Robert M. Travis
1926-1927	John H. Mahurin
1927	Harry L. Neel, Jr.
1927-1929	William Thomas Feland
1929-1930	Isaac S. Holmes
1930-1931	Glenn E. Baker
1931-1937	William B. Hollingshead
1937-1940	L.M. (Dan) McCandless
1940-1942	Forbes Barrett
1942-1943	William Thomas Feland
1943-1951	Kirk Higginbotham
1951-1956	Frank P. McCaslin
1956-1968	Harold English
1968-1978	Richard Long
1978-1980	William J. Anthony
1980-1988	Joseph Centeno
1988-1992	Russell R. Mathews
1992-1998	Dan Shiner
1998-2003	John I. Sterling
2003-2012	Danny Macagni
2012-2017	Ralph Martin
2017-2020	Phil Hansen
2021-	Marc Schneider

Chapter 10: Misdemeanors

Misdemeanor comes from the word "demeanor," which means "behavior toward others. "Mis" refers to wrong or bad so *misdemeanor* literally means "bad behavior toward others." In law, a "misdemeanor" is "a crime less serious than a felony." California law defines a misdemeanor as a crime for which the maximum sentence is no more than one year in county jail. California misdemeanors fall into two categories: "standard" misdemeanors, punishable by up to six months in jail and/or a fine of up to $1,000; and "Gross" or "aggravated" misdemeanors, punishable by up to 364 days in jail and/or a fine of up to $1,000 or more.

Common "standard" misdemeanors include (but are not limited to):

    Drug possession
    Drunk in public
    Indecent Exposure (1st offense)
    Petty theft
    Prostitution
    Shoplifting
    Trespassing

Common "aggravated" misdemeanors include (but are not limited to):

    Domestic battery
    Driving on a suspended license
    DUI without injury
    Violating a restraining order

MAN HELD TO ANSWER CHARGE OF DISTURBING PEACE

A. L. Rossie was arrested yesterday by Chief of Police Ramsey for using profane language, under the influence of liquor, in the city streets before women and children. Rossie was arrested recently in Santa Barbara for bootlegging in Los Angeles and was ordered not to return to this community. He was charged yesterday with disturbing the peace and was held to answer today before Judge L. J. Morris.

Boys Accused of Indecent Exposure

Siguro Otto Ness, of Orcutt, posted $100 bond Saturday night shortly after his arrest on Highway 101 near the Beacon Motel on charges of drunk driving. The arrest was made by Highway Patrolman V. N. Bailey and J. D. Daly.

Faustino Segovia Alaniz, an employe of the Rosemary Farms, and a juvenile companion were arrested in Moose Hall Saturday night on charges of indecent exposure. Alaniz posted $25 bond.

Paul Quesada Silva of Guadalupe, was arrested in the 800 block on West Main last night charged with being drunk and disturbing the peace.

c. 1941

L. A. MAN SENTENCED

Sydney George Schwartz, 29, Los Angeles, was sentenced Monday in Justice Court to 15 days in the city jail on a charge that he tried to steal several avacados from Leo's Drive Inn on N. Broadway early Monday morning. He pleaded guilty to the charge.

DRUNK IN CAR

Robert Fay Tulloch, 48, 313 W. Park Ave., was arrested and booked in city jail Monday night for being intoxicated in a car. He was found by police about 11:30 p.m. in the 700 block on E. Orange Street. He posted $10 bail and is to appear in Justice Court on June 26 at 11 a.m.

THEFT OF CHANGE

Mary Hernandez, owner of the Sanitary Self-Service Automatic Laundry, 700 W. Cook St., reported to police Monday the theft of $59.60 in change from a coin changer machine. There was no evidence of forced entry into the machine, according to police reports.

Youth Admits to Orgy In S.M. Mausoleum

The senseless, wanton destruction wrought by vandals Dec. 10 at the Santa Maria Cemetery, 730 E. Stowell Rd. was cleared up this morning by a 20-year-old boy currently in Santa Barbara County jail awaiting probation hearing for another crime.

City Police Captain Lloyd Britell said this morning that Arthur Moore, 20, has admitted throwing a beer party in the cemetery mausoleum during which a number of delicately blue colored stained glass windows were destroyed.

Moore said his companions on that night were a 19 year old boy, and a 17 year old girl. During the course of the beer-bust they got drunk, and he and the other boy started throwing bottles and other objects through the windows.

Britell said the two implicated by Moore have admitted nothing. The girl is already on probation from another offense, he stated.

Just 11 days after the orgy in the mausoleum, Moore was shot in the chest by Overland Private Patrol officer Bruno Zemaitis who spotted Moore and two others in the act of burglarizing Nicely's Market, 2360 S. Broadway.

Moore is awaiting probation hearing following his admission of that crime, as is Delmar L. Gilchrist who also admitted taking part in the market burglary. The third youth, a juvenile, has been turned over to juvenile officials.

At the mausoleum four windows were destroyed, and two others badly damaged. They were installed when the mausoleum was built in 1914, and are irreplaceable.

Moore said Dec. 10 was not the first time a party had been held at the cemetery. In fact, the night before the windows were destroyed a party was attended by a "whole flock" of people, he said.

c. 1963

Dog Stolen

Theft of a Boston bulldog from his car while it was parked in the 100 block of North Broadway last night was reported to police by R. H. Robinson, 221 East Chapel.

November 1941

Women Forfeit Bonds

Rosemary Osborn, 38, Monterey Park, forfeited $15 bail on a charge of being drunk and disturbing the peace in the Victory Cafe.

Bail was also forfeited by Fay Walker, 33, Lompoc, charged with being drunk and disturbing the peace in the 100 block on East Main. She forfeited $15.

Filamon Recendez Mesa, 33, a Mexican laborer, charged with being drunk and disturbing the peace in the 100 block on East Main, was given a sentence of six months in jail, suspended on condition of good behavior for a year.

August 1944

A Stroll in the Night — 31 March 59

NINE-YEAR-OLD NAILED ON STREET WITH "GUN"

A nine-year-old "Dan'l Boone", who got his shootin' iron and ammo the hard way, had his adventures chopped short early this morning.

The Vandenberg AFB runaway was nabbed by police officers on Broadway about 2:45 a.m. as he sauntered casually along with a BB gun tucked under his arm.

A few minutes earlier, the boy tossed a rock through the glass door of Simas Sportings Goods, 231 E. Main St. Crawling through the hole, he helped himself to the gun, several boxes of BB's, a pocket knife, flashing and a compass.

Just in case bear huntin' was scarce, he also snitched several roll of mints to ease his hunger.

Merchant Patrolman Bruno Zemaitis spotted the boy and called police, who had found the breakin some time earlier. All the loot was in his pockets.

Police said this is the third time the boy has been picked up after running away from his home. He was handed over to the probation department for questioning.

Epilogue

Historically speaking, crime is a fascination for many. The stories of our ancestors really shows that nothing is new under the sun. We are all human. We live, we die and, along the way, we make mistakes. There's no judgement intended in any of the cases presented.

Crime Scene Cleanup

"When tragedy strikes — whether it's a homicide, suicide, unattended death, trauma, or blood spill, Crime Scene Clean Up is there to help you through it. We have provided trauma cleanup services to Santa-Maria families and businesses for over 20 years."

References

Websites
  americancowboychronicles.com
  Ancestry.com
  CityofSantaMaria.org
  Findagrave.com
  Fold3.com
  morro-bay.com
  Newspapers.com
  Pinterest.com
  Wikipedia.org

Books
  <u>This is Our Valley</u> by Vada F. Carlson
  <u>Stagecoach Days</u> by Walker A. Tompkins
  <u>For the Good of the Country</u> by Hattie Stone Benefield
  <u>Rolling Stone</u> by O.W. Maulsby

Periodicals
  Daily Bee, November 1860
  Lompoc Record
  San Francisco Examiner, July 1901
  San Luis Tribune
  Santa Barbara Independent
  Santa Maria Daily Times
  Santa Maria Times
  Tulare Advance-Register
  Visalia Weekly Sun, November 1860

Organizations
  California Department of Corrections and Rehabilitation
  Santa Maria Valley Historical Society and Museum
  San Diego History Center

www.ingramcontent.com/pod-product-compliance
Lightning Source LLC
Chambersburg PA
CBHW081218230426
43666CB00015B/2789